Baseball
for the Utterly
CONFUSED

Ed Randall

Mc Graw Hill

New York Chicago San Francisco Lisbon London Madrid Mexico City
Milan New Delhi San Juan Seoul Singapore Sydney Toronto

1 2 3 4 5 6 7 8 9 10 11 12 13 14 15 16   WFR/WFR   1 9 8 7 6 5 4 3 2 1 0

ISBN   978-0-07-163474-8
MHID   0-07-163474-6

McGraw-Hill books are available at special quantity discounts to use as premiums and sales promotions or for use in corporate training programs. To contact a representative, please e-mail us at bulksales@mcgraw-hill.com.

All my thanks go to Big Ed and Nora and her eternal radiance—for thinking me up, on whose shoulders I stand, and who are my life's aspiration and collective inspiration. There is not a day I don't hold myself up for measure to their yardstick. As my center of gravity and sanctuary, they devoted their lives in building a foundation of boundless love, kindness, and joy through the light of their incandescent spirit. I have often said I am all that I am because of them and I am only half the person each of them was. But I'm still tryin'.

And to Joey—for the smiles and laughs he brings me every day, for leaning his head on my feet under the desk as I wrote and for putting his heart into everything and setting an example that inspired me. To look at him, I knew everything would turn out just fine.

Contents

Preface   vii

Introduction: For the Love of the Game   1

Chapter 1   Rules of the Game   13

Chapter 2   Momentous Moments—from the Beginning Through
             World War II (1823–1945)   27

Chapter 3   Batter Up—the Art of Hitting   39

Chapter 4   Momentous Moments—the Golden Age of Baseball
             (1946–1957)   53

Chapter 5   The Art of Pitching—a Comprehensive Lesson
             (So, Heads Up)   65

Chapter 6   Momentous Moments—Expansion (1958–1967)   83

Chapter 7   Managerial Strategies   97

Chapter 8   Momentous Moments—Divisional Play (1968–1975)   117

Chapter 9   Stats—Keeping Score, Sabermetrics, and Fantasy Baseball   131

Chapter 10   Momentous Moments—the Dawn and Rise of Free Agency
              (1976–1993)   151

Chapter 11   Defining and Climbing the Standings   185

Chapter 12   Momentous Moments—the Wild-Card Era (1994–Present)   193

Index   225

Preface

◆◆

I lived in Spanish Harlem until fire claimed our home and we moved to the Bronx. (Attention, all New York City tour buses: add 660 Riverside Drive to your itinerary.)

My parents, in their infinite wisdom, enrolled me in the University Heights Little League.

The year was 1962.

I was the kid in right field playing for the Bears. They played me in right field because it was against the rules to play me in Sweden.

I would be out there counting dandelions. If, heaven forbid, a fly ball would be hit my way, I would begin jumping up and down like a pogo stick and hope the ball would not come down and hit me on the head.

Clueless.

I might as well have worn a bowling shoe on the end of my arm rather than a glove. Funny thing, I did not receive a postcard inviting me to rejoin the following year.

Who knew that it would turn out to be my walk year?

That year off, baseball really kicked in for me. I spent it teaching myself how to pitch. I was back with the Lions the following year and, armed with an "I'll-show-you" attitude, made the all-star team.

Another all-star season as a pitcher was in the stars a couple years later despite the fact that I hit only .108, with three hits all season, two of them bunts. Then, as now, I would refer to myself as the first "switch-batter": I could definitely swing the bat from both sides of the plate, but a *hitter* I wasn't. I'd inevitably get the take sign on a 3-and-2 count. I'd look down at the third-base coach to check the sign, and he'd just look back at me with his palms up and shrug.

I ate, drank, and slept baseball. My fabulous Italian mother would say, "Edwin, baseball is an *obsession*!"

In later years, why study trigonometry when you can be sitting in the back of the classroom figuring out Tom Seaver's earned run average?

Someone had to do this. If not me, then who, for goodness' sake? (Because I was so busy figuring out Seaver's earned run average, I was excused by the Irish Christian Brothers from enjoying a summer filled with baseball so I could attend summer school for trigonometry.)

I am proud to say that my ability improved to the point where, weeks after graduating from high school (*which didn't have a baseball team!*), I had a tryout with the Kansas City Royals.

How many people can say that?

Introduction

For the Love of the Game

◆◆◆◆◆◆◆◆◆◆◆◆◆◆◆◆◆◆◆◆◆◆◆◆◆◆◆◆◆◆◆◆◆◆

Let's eliminate any utter confusion.

I know that you know that you just can't get enough of this game, so welcome, as we satisfy your craving for all things baseball and cover it in context and with perspective.

Here are our articles of faith.

For 162 games every year, we believe in miracles. It's baseball, and that's why millions will be sitting in the gray glare of a television set or listening on radio or the World Wide Web just as you likely are now, while the game is being played, waiting to see what's gonna happen next.

And when it happens, you still won't believe it.

That's baseball. It's your dream repository; it keeps you warm at night; it's part of who we are—the background music of America.

It's the only game you can follow on the radio, the perfect game.

Practically every man, woman, and child knows this game and has watched his or her chosen heroes. We all wanted to be them.

This is our game, the game we love, filled with cultural landmarks that punctuate our lives and surely resonate.

At the ballyard, you forget all your cares. In a world of fear and trembling, we hold fast to what remains constant and are grateful for a pastime worthy of our lifelong connection.

In the sanctuary of the ballpark, we are always safe at home. It is our heritage, part of the soul, culture, and fabric of this country.

Baseball is the game that marks time, where the past is always present. It's the grand cathedral of sports.

Baseball is America's great secular religion. It reflects who we are and what we aspire to be. It is an expression of our culture.

Mystic cords bind us to baseball, keeping the generations sewn together.

We love the symmetry of the layout of the field, how the game unfolds in a linear fashion in which one thing leads to another that leads to another, and the fact that you can go to the ballpark for years and, on any given day, see something you've never seen before.

"The majority of American males put themselves to sleep by striking out the batting order of the New York Yankees," James Thurber wrote more than half a century ago.

Not much has changed since then.

Baseball, for all its well-documented problems off the field, remains a labor of love on the field for a good portion of American boys and men who aspire to or fantasize about playing the game. Or, they recall having played the game, and playing it well, sometimes better than big leaguers—for it is a law of geriatrics that the older you get, the faster you could run, the farther you hit the ball, and the harder you pitched as a boy. Meanwhile, the growing number of female fans, spurred to a significant degree by their expanding participation in softball, also contribute to the popularity of the game.

The game is so good, so compelling, so much a part of us—a linkage that goes back to the Civil War—that it thrives almost miraculously.

History demonstrates that America is smitten with baseball, for all its faults. No divorce is imminent.

The World Series is a yearly reminder that October is when baseball is the best game of all.

Not the industry of baseball. Not the high finance of baseball, as in the multimillion-dollar contracts for some players. Not the arrogance of baseball, as in the behavior of some players and owners.

Simply the game of baseball.

Three strikes. Four balls. Ninety feet between bases, 60 feet 6 inches to the pitcher's mound. Three outs. Nine innings, if not a few more innings every so often.

Most important, no clock!

Without the clock that confines football, basketball, and hockey games to so many minutes, a baseball game never expires until the final out, no matter what the score.

Baseball Always Provides Hope

Some people think baseball is dull, and during the long season, it often is. (The great writer Red Smith once wrote, "Baseball is dull only to those with dull minds.") But it's not dull in October, not in the World Series.

It's dull sometimes in April or May or June or July or August or even in September in a game between two teams with no chance of qualifying for the play-offs. The interminable stare-down between a pitcher and a batter. The wait for the arrival of a relief pitcher. The hitter's constant stepping out of the batter's box. The manager's chess moves. The pace between innings.

But those same situations that sometimes make it dull during the season always make it better in October.

It's considered a team game, but the continual confrontation between the pitcher and the batter makes it an individual game within a team game. That continual one-on-one does not exist in football, basketball, and hockey.

Baseball's playing surface is also much larger than those of other sports. The larger the surface, the higher the potential for the unexpected.

The game is so good that it survives the stupidity of its schism over the designated hitter, especially in the World Series. Only baseball could get away with having two different games within one game.

Yes, baseball takes longer than it seems it should. During the season, that can be a bore, but in a close game in October, the hours only heighten the tension, because there's no clock ticking off the minutes and the seconds.

It's not like that in other sports.

In football, is there anything more dull than a Super Bowl quarterback taking the snap and kneeling to run out the clock in the final minutes? In basketball, is there anything more dull than a losing team fouling simply to prolong the agony? In hockey, is there anything more dull than a winning team icing the puck to protect a lead?

In baseball, no clock means no kneeling, no fouls, no icing. No clock means a team always has a chance to win.

Sometimes that chance is remote, as the Pittsburgh Pirates realized after losing three games in the 1960 World Series to the Yankees by scores of 16–3, 10–0, and 12–0. But that chance was still there until the Yankees got the 27th out.

Bill Mazeroski didn't allow them to when he became the only player in baseball history to end the seventh game of the World Series with a home run.

Time didn't run out. It never does.

That's baseball. That's why, in October, it's the best game.

No matter how hard they try, the people who run baseball cannot destroy this great game.

They can shut it down for months on end with strikes and lockouts. They can even cancel the World Series, casually walking away from their biggest showcase. And baseball survives.

They can dilute the product with expanded play-offs and wild-card teams, gimmickry borrowed from basketball, football, and hockey. And baseball survives.

They can order postseason games to be played in the middle of the night at the end of October (or, in the case of 2009, early November), guaranteeing dwindling audiences and frigid temperatures. And, baseball survives.

At every turn, they test the sport's resiliency, challenging it to overcome one burden after another. Arrogant players demanding to be paid for autographs and forgetting simple, common courtesy, issuing statements instead of sitting still for interviews.

Owners looking for new ways to extort a few extra stadium and tax concessions from their cities.

And still baseball survives.

They regionalized play-off telecasts, hiding half their postseason games from large sections of the country. They played with different rules in different cities—10 players here, 9 there—and switched from one network to another in the middle of each postseason series.

And baseball still survives.

This wonderful game defies all odds, simply because of the way it was designed.

There's no 24-second clock to rush the action here. The game does not count seconds and minutes, leaving plenty of time for the drama to build.

So, there's time to contemplate the interleague showdown between Roy Halladay, the best pitcher in the game, and Albert Pujols, the best slugger. How will Halladay, a Picasso of pitching, choose to neutralize Pujols's brooding raw power? Work the corners of the plate? Keep it down and away in the strike zone? Maybe up and in? Let's see.

In basketball, there is no time to think about how LeBron James will attack Kobe Bryant. Spend a moment to think it over and the ball is going in the other direction.

In football, a defensive lineman lines up and takes off after Eli Manning. It begins and ends in the blink of an eye. In 10 blinks of an eye, Halladay is still thinking over how to pitch to Pujols.

In hockey, Alex Ovetchkin shoots in a flash, and Martin Brodeur either stops it or doesn't. By then, Halladay may have the sign from the catcher.

Too slow for you? Hey, it took some time to paint the Sistine Chapel, too, but it was a worthwhile endeavor.

There is nothing wrong with baseball. There never has been.

Baseball is a bonding sport.

"It is an endless game of repeated summers, joining the long generations of all the fathers and all the sons," poet Donald Hall wrote in "Fathers Playing Catch with Sons."

The late baseball commissioner A. Bartlett Giamatti once wrote, "Baseball breaks your heart. It is designed to break your heart."

This Renaissance scholar, Princeton professor, president of Yale, and lifelong Boston Red Sox fan was asked how someone of his intelligence and sophistication could forsake a career in academia to become commissioner of baseball. The implication was that he had walked out of a dinner at the White House to dine at a roadside greasy spoon.

"There are a lot of people who know me who can't for the life of them understand why I would do something as meaningless as baseball," Giamatti said. After a brief silence, he looked up and said simply, "If only they knew."

Yes, if they only knew.

Giamatti, the son of an Italian professor, had the words of several languages at his command. He could summon the wit and wisdom of generations to speak on grave issues of the world. Yet, when it came to explaining his love for a game, he was mute. He was at a loss for words because there are no words to describe the passion of baseball. And that is what it is: a passion.

No less a passion than what a zealot feels for religion. Or a parent for a child.

Emotions defy description, and baseball, unlike any other sport, is an emotion. Not a game of emotions, like hockey or football or basketball. Simply an emotion. A love. A passion.

Throughout history, poets and songwriters have struggled to describe their loves. They can portray the beauty they see but not the love they feel.

It is a thing of beauty to watch a home run struck high on an arc into the night sky. The gentle sheen of a miniature moon rising steadily against the backdrop of gray-black. A neon yellow foul pole lurking somewhere just on the edge of vision. The glare of stadium lights coming back into focus as the ball reaches apogee—testing the limits of man's strength against nature—and then begins its unstoppable fall back to Earth.

It is magnificent, too, to watch something as simple as a lazy fly ball to right field. To watch the second baseman rush onto the outfield grass, right hand pointed high overhead, yelling to help a teammate make the play.

Or the comforting crescent of gold and emerald where the infield meets the outfield, the border between one world and another, between groundouts and singles.

All these and more—much, much more—are part of the timeless beauty of baseball. Tiny capsules of why the game is special, why it endures.

But the beauty of baseball is one thing. The love of it is another.

Words will never convey the profound passions kindled by something as simple as the sound of a fastball nestling comfortably into a mitt, or the sight of a newly chalked batter's box waiting to be trampled.

Giamatti was right.

If only they knew.

Baseball Is Eternal

Season after season is painted over on our memory of the game. Only a fool would try to scrape anything away. Baseball itself has changed far less than, say, basketball or football, and compared with the rest of American life, it has hardly changed at all.

We have changed. Through television, we learned it was not necessary to actually attend a game to take pleasure in baseball. And then, in a far more radical discovery, we found pleasure in a fantasy version of baseball, a fantasy that used and distorted the reality of baseball.

Baseball's past is this: We sit in Yankee Stadium rooting for Derek Jeter, C. C. Sabathia, Mark Teixeira, and Mariano Rivera to thrill us and justify our adoration and their salaries.

Baseball's present is this: We sit at home with computerized data on every major-league player's statistical performance. Jeter, Sabathia, Teixeira, and Rivera are mathematical objects on fantasy teams. Whatever human chemistry flows among them is irrelevant. However they might lift each other's potential to win or lose is gone.

Baseball's future is this: We combine the past pleasure of rooting for a real team that someone else owns with the present pleasure of rooting for statistics that make up a team we own. In that future, we will share ownership of the real Yankees, and we will make and lose money.

Baseball has always been whatever you make of it.

Baseball is about those magic moments in which you feel immortal, whether you were the fat kid in right field or a Cy Young Award winner.

This happened 42 years ago:

I was the ace of the Holy Family Club team in the senior division of the University Heights Little League. It was a Saturday-morning game just before the end of the season in early June at Inwood Park, at the northern tip of upper Manhattan, that began at 8:30. The opposition was a good team, the Holy Name Society, another organization sponsored by my parish, Saint Nicholas of Tolentine.

I was 15 years old and barely awake. Never did get the hang of warming up at 8:15 in the morning, and if my wildest dreams were still percolating, what lay ahead was not a part of that.

I don't have the box score, but I remember we were the visiting team, because I took a lead to the bottom of the seventh.

Before 11 A.M. had rolled around, 16 of the 21 outs I had recorded were strikeouts, a UHLL senior division record. The roundhouse curve was working, and I even got Joe Vielandi, this big, strapping athletic guy who was once a grammar school classmate, three times.

It was my best day ever.

And how many of us even get that much?

Every pitch was a perfect strike, as if I were walking the ball over the plate. The ball danced and the ball hummed. It gives me shivers to remember how live my arm felt that morning. When the game was over, I wasn't drained and could have gone back out there for more. I never came that close again. I'll tell you this, though: you can have all the cybersport fantasies you want, but that exhilarating feeling that June morning and all its variations is the reason why baseball will never die.

Since the University Heights Little League is but a memory, I proudly hold that record in perpetuity.

Put it on my tombstone.

How many people have just that one special day? I think about that game every time I look down and see that field while crossing a nearby bridge.

In our own way, as fans, we have a greater vested interest in baseball than some of those principals in the inner sanctum. After all, we pour so many hours and dollars into making baseball the industry it is today. Our passion is free of charge, and if it meant in the day smuggling a transistor radio into math class every October or developing a mysterious cough that kept us out of school on the morning of game seven, so what? What matters more now: the lesson we might have missed or the perfect game Don Larsen threw against Brooklyn when we had the intuition to revise our schedules to accommodate baseball?

Dale Mitchell went down looking for the final out; Yogi Berra ran to Larsen and jumped into his arms. Face it: you never would have forgiven yourself if you were doing geometry at that special moment. You haven't had much use for angles and triangles since, but whenever you see Yogi, you remember how baseball reached out and grabbed you decades ago.

It can happen when you least expect it. It's many years later, and I have never forgiven myself—and never will—for walking out of Yankee Stadium after reporting on the field with Albert Belle of all people during batting practice on the Saturday of Labor Day weekend in 1993, before Jim Abbott went out and threw his no-hitter against Cleveland—Jim Abbott, *my all-time favorite sports hero*, *that* Jim Abbott.

There was no turning your back on the game then, nor should there be now. That means loving it even if, at times, it doesn't seem to love you and yours anymore. No amount of war between them and us can destroy the peace between you and your drive along with Vin Scully or any of the other generational gods of baseball broadcasting speaking to you from the dashboard of your car.

He and his contemporaries introduced you to this lifelong affair, and you followed up faithfully by devouring every newspaper clipping the next day. And you were hooked.

Then and now, you and yours, including future generations that look like you, flipping dials, checking scorecards, and scanning schedules on the Net to see what team is coming to town on that summer afternoon you know will be sunny and warm. The family game isn't going any-where. Its perfect symmetry shall endure, its sounds and smells won't perish, and all the beasts in the world can't ruin the beauty of a green diamond.

What we have here is an American institution of immeasurable worth to the public.

CHAPTER 1
Rules of the Game

◆◆◆◆◆◆◆◆◆◆◆◆◆◆◆◆◆◆◆◆◆◆◆◆◆◆◆◆◆◆◆◆◆◆◆◆◆◆

Let's start with the basics. Two teams of at least nine players, led by a manager (usually dressed in uniform, in charge of the players and several supporting coaches—hitting, pitching, bullpen, first-base, and third-base, among others), will play each other for a minimum of five innings. Each team's objective is to win the game by outscoring its opponent. (Hello! Please tell me you already knew this and weren't that utterly confused!)

Sounds simple, right?

Three things to consider right off the bat:

1. That team of 9 is sometimes a team of 10, as the designated hitter has unfortunately taken root in much of the baseball world outside of the National League (more on the atrocity that is the DH later). Major-league rosters also have a bench, a rotation, and a bullpen, for 25 total players in uniform and eligible to play. A typical alignment would include nine position players, five starting pitchers, and six to seven relief pitchers (including a long man, capable of pitching several innings; specialists for lefty and righty batters; a closer, charged with shutting the door on the opposing team in its final at bat; and, ideally, one or two setup men, capable of maintaining a lead and acting as a bridge between the starter and the closer). The other five players might include a DH or power bat to come off the bench in key moments, a backup catcher (squatting for nine-plus innings as foul balls and bar-

reling base runners bounce off your body takes a toll on the starting catcher, making backup a must—especially for day games after night games), a utility infielder (capable of playing multiple positions), and a fourth outfielder (in case of injury, as a defensive replacement, or as an additional pinch hitter). Of those four to five bench spots, general managers will try to ensure that among them they have both lefty and righty bats, to counter the pitching moves of opposing managers, as well as a player with speed, in case a pinch runner is called for.

2. The number of innings played is dependent on the level of play, the score, and the weather. Everyone knows that a major-league baseball game is nine innings long (eight and a half if the home team is winning going into the bottom of the ninth), but Little League games can be six to seven innings. Tie games usually go extra innings (more on that in a moment).

Then there's the matter of an official game. In major-league baseball, a game is official after five innings (four and a half if the home team has a lead going into the bottom of the fifth). So, if the heavens open up after five innings have been played, and there's no sign of the rain's ever ending, the team with the lead can get the win. If fewer than five innings are in the books, and there's no chance of the game's being resumed, then it's a do-over, to be played again some other day (meaning that the stats recorded during those first four innings will never find their way into the record book—just ask Roger Maris . . . more on him later).

It gets complicated when rain or some other circumstance either stops a tied game or stops a game in which a tie has just been broken. If, let's say, after five innings of play the visiting team pulls ahead in the top of the sixth, and before the home team can play three outs' worth of baseball in the bottom half of the same inning, Noah gets on the PA system to tell the lucky fans in attendance that his ark is parked in section G of the lot out back and is about to set sail, then the top half of the inning is scrubbed from the box score, and the game reverts back to where it was at the end of the last full inning of play. As the game was tied at that point (or if the scenario didn't play out exactly as described and a tied game was stopped), the game could be suspended, to be completed at a future date.

 Joel Hanrahan, a National League pitcher, once recorded a win on a day he wasn't even playing, for a team he was no longer with! Hanrahan was pitching for the Nationals in a game against the Astros when it was suspended. Two months later, the game resumed, the Nats won, and Hanrahan was awarded the "W" even though he had been traded to the Pirates in between and had the night off.

3. While major-league baseball is designed to be played until a team ends an inning with a lead (the 2002 All-Star Game and spring training exhibitions notwithstanding), college baseball and other leagues have produced ties on occasion.

The Field

The baseball diamond is configured with 90 feet between consecutive bases, 60 feet 6 inches (and 10 inches off the ground) separating the pitcher's mound from home plate, and 127 feet 3⅜ inches from home plate to second base and from first base to third base. The MLB rules also suggest that "the line from home base through the pitcher's plate to second base shall run East-Northwest." See Figure 1.1.

The rest of the field consists of boxes for the batter, for the catcher, and for the first- and third-base coaches, as well as a designated area for the on-deck batter. Foul lines run from home plate through first and third base, and the distances that each one spans (along with the fences in the outfield) vary from park to park (but can be no less than 250 feet at the major-league level). MLB does recommend approximately 320 feet down the line and 400 feet to center field, with 60 feet or more separating home plate and the infield from the stands.

Figure 1.1

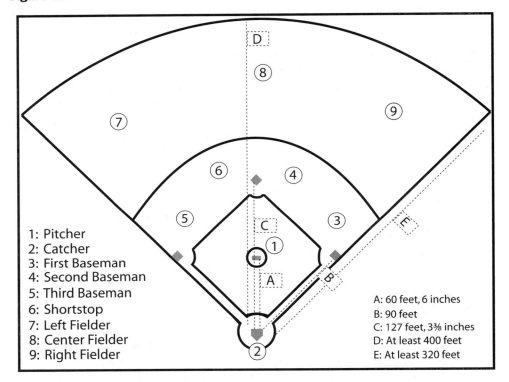

1: Pitcher
2: Catcher
3: First Baseman
4: Second Baseman
5: Third Baseman
6: Shortstop
7: Left Fielder
8: Center Fielder
9: Right Fielder

A: 60 feet, 6 inches
B: 90 feet
C: 127 feet, 3⅜ inches
D: At least 400 feet
E: At least 320 feet

Home plate is a pentagon that measures 17 inches across the front (the width of the strike zone), with two sides at right angles to the front measuring 8½ inches and two sides connecting the foul lines and completing the diamond at 12 inches each.

Talking Baseball

Baseball has a language all its own, and to understand the sport and its rules, you'll need to be able to talk the talk before you can walk the walk. Here are some of the terms you'll hear while watching a game, along with their definitions.

Balk. The balk rule prevents pitchers from trying to be too sneaky when it comes to runners on base. It basically states that a pitcher is not allowed to do anything that would be considered disruptive to his motion. A balk is typically called when a pitcher either fails to come to a complete stop before delivering the baseball home (the stop indicates the beginning of the actual pitch) or fails to step off the mound before checking the runner (throwing to a base). When a balk is committed, each runner advances one base.

Ball. Any given pitch is, for the most part, a strike or a ball (with some rarities and exceptions as noted later). A ball is a pitch outside of the strike zone at which the batter does not swing. It is the first number in a standard count, so at 3–2, the batter has three balls and two strikes on him—four balls produce a walk. (I threw many of these in my amateur career. Whereas the great control pitchers could, as they say in the game, hit a gnat in the butt, I was the opposite.)

Base Coach. Each team has two uniformed base coaches while the team is up at bat, a first-base coach and a third-base coach. The base coaches direct the runners.

The third-base coach relays the signs from the manager to the hitter and runners. The first-base coach's responsibilities are pretty much confined to patting runners on the butt, reminding them how many outs there are, and bending over and picking up discarded equipment that was used at bat.

Base on Balls. Also known as a walk and abbreviated BB. When a pitcher delivers four balls outside of the strike zone during any at bat, the batter is awarded first base. (As with Warren Buffett, I gave out *many* awards in my time.)

Battery. The battery comprises the pitcher and the catcher—who are sometimes referred to as "battery mates" when spoken of as a pair.

Bunt. In key situations, instead of swinging for the fences, a batter might square off, face the pitcher with his bat out in front of him, and tap the ball so it takes a slow roll along the infield. Bunting the ball is an effective way to advance a runner (giving up an out to get your man from first to second base or from second to third) or take advantage of an unprepared fielder.

Catcher's Box. This is the area behind home plate designated for the catcher while a pitch is being delivered.

Catcher's Interference. If the catcher's glove gets in the way of the batter's swing, and contact is made, "catcher's interference" is called and the batter is awarded first base.

Dead Ball. This term applies both to an era of play early in the game in which the ball was less tightly wound and to the temporary suspension of action when a ball is legally out of play.

Doubleheader. Affectionately referred to as a twin bill, the traditional doubleheader was two games played back-to-back, for a single admission. (This is a quaint concept that has pretty much gone the way of the dodo bird because of unmitigated greed on the part of players and owners.) More often than not, today's doubleheaders are the results of postponements and are played as "day-night doubleheaders," in which the stands are cleared between games and a second set of ticket holders is ushered in for the nightcap.

Double Play. "The pitcher's best friend," a double play occurs when two offensive players are called out during an uninterrupted (and error-free) sequence of events.

Fair Ball. When contact is made, a batted ball is either fair or foul. If the ball first lands in fair territory, is in fair territory while crossing first or third base, or makes contact with anything in fair territory (including players, umpires, the bases, and the foul poles), it is ruled fair.

If you lay down a bunt along the first-base line and it spins foul, it is a foul ball if nobody has touched it. Otherwise, run like hell! Conversely, if you're playing first base and the batter hits a pop fly to you in fair territory and, like a dope, you drop it and the ball rolls into foul territory, that is a fair ball, and you will have to eat your lunch all by yourself.

Fair Territory. This is the field between (and including) the foul lines, going up the outfield wall and extending vertically through each foul pole. Fair territory also includes the bases.

Repeat after me, class: All foul lines are in fair territory. Thus, if a bunted ball goes to die on the chalk of the third-base line, that's a hit!

Fielder's Choice. When, on a fair ground ball, a fielder decides to attempt a play on a runner already on base instead of going after the batter by attempting the play at first, the batter who reaches first is not credited with a hit.

One of the basic tenets of playing defense is to get the lead runner. So, if there are runners at first and second with fewer than two outs, and a ground ball is hit near the third-base bag, the third baseman would field the ball and run to the bag to force out the lead runner. Still, he has a choice as to what to do with the ball and which base runner he will go after. Thus, it's a fielder's choice.

Force Play. On a fair ball, the batter has a right to first base. If a runner is on first at the time, he must advance, and if the defense gets the ball to second base ahead of him, he is out. Similarly, if there are runners on first and second (or if the bases are loaded), and the batter makes fair contact, then each runner must advance to clear the base he was occupying.

A force can be removed during a play if the trailing runner is called out. When a batter flies out, there is no force, as there is no trail runner who must be accommodated. Also, if, with a runner on first, a ground ball is hit to the first baseman, who steps on the bag, the batter is out and the force no longer applies to the existing base runner. If that runner had attempted to advance to second on contact, throwing the ball to the base ahead of him would no longer be enough to get him out. With no force in effect, he would need to be tagged off the base to be called out. In this situation, many fielders will attempt to throw the ball to second base first and have whoever receives the ball at second throw it back to the player covering first, to preserve force-outs at both ends of the double play.

Foul Ball. When contact is made, a batted ball is either fair or foul. If the ball first lands in foul territory, is in foul territory while crossing first or third base, or makes contact with anything in foul territory (including players, umpires, base coaches, and other objects on the field), it is ruled foul.

A foul ball is also a strike against the hitter, unless there are already two strikes. With two strikes, a batter may keep his at bat alive by fouling off pitches; however, a caught foul tip is still a strike.

A fly ball is ruled fair or foul based on the position of the ball in relation to the foul line, not on where the fielder is when he touches it. So, a player cannot stand in foul territory and swat down a ball clearly on a path to land on the other side of the foul line. Thinking about that last part of the rule, you may ask yourself why a player would even consider swatting a ball when he could just catch it. The only situation I can think of in which this part of the rule could ever realistically come into play is if a fly ball was hit to either corner outfielder with a runner on third prepared to tag up, and rather than giving the opposition a chance to score, the outfielder tries to get clever by having the ball declared foul.

The one strange exception to the "object in fair territory" portion of the fair/foul ruling concerns the pitcher's mound. According to the rules: "A batted ball not touched by a fielder, which hits the pitcher's rubber and rebounds into foul territory, between home and first, or between home and third base is a foul ball."

Foul Tip. If a batter grazes a pitch, and it is still caught by the catcher, it is a foul tip. Any foul tip that is legally caught (before touching the ground) is a strike.

Illegal Pitch. If a pitcher delivers a pitch but fails to maintain contact between his pivot foot and the pitcher's mound, it is an illegal pitch. Similarly, if a pitcher tries a "quick pitch" to somehow fool the batter or catch him off guard, it is also illegal. When a pitcher delivers an illegal pitch with runners on base, a balk is called.

Infield Fly. When there are runners on first and second or when the bases are loaded, with fewer than two outs, and a fly ball (as opposed to an attempted bunt or a line drive) is, in the umpire's opinion, easily playable for an infielder, the "infield fly rule" is invoked. This means that the batter is out regardless of whether the ball is caught or dropped (unless the ball is dropped and bounces foul before reaching first or third base, in which case it is called foul). The rule is called to protect the runners, as a dropped ball would create multiple force-play opportunities.

Regardless of what happens to the ball, nothing changes in relation to the fly ball and the runners. They must still wait until it is caught (if it is caught) to attempt to advance.

The infield fly rule is one of the game's oddest. Say I'm playing third base, and the opposition has the bases loaded with fewer than two out. The batter then lifts a pop fly to me. As the ball is in the air, the supervising umpire will call him out. It doesn't matter if I catch the ball or not. I can even let it drop or have the ball fall out of my glove—the batter is still out. The runners can run at their own risk. The problem with letting the ball drop is that it could hit something and bounce away, allowing the runners to score easily. My advice: don't get cute; just catch the ball.

Interference. There are four categories of interference: offensive, defensive, umpire's, and spectator (fan).

Offensive interference is called when the team at bat goes out of its way to somehow obstruct, impede, or confuse a fielder while in the act of making a play. This infraction may be called on an overaggressive base runner who attempts a hard slide into second base, trying to knock down a fielder and break up a potential double play, where it is ruled that the slide was too far out of the baseline. When offensive interference is called, the runner on whom it was called is out, and other runners are instructed to return to the last base they occupied prior to the interference, per the umpire's judgment.

Defensive interference is called when a fielder in some manner gets in the way of a batter trying to hit a pitch. (While the culprit is often the catcher, this infraction could also be called on a charging infielder in a bunt situation.) *Umpire's interference* is called either when an ump somehow disrupts a catcher attempting to throw out a potential base stealer or when an ump gets hit with a fair ball in fair territory before the ball passes a fielder. *Spectator* or *fan interference* is called when someone in the stands reaches out to the field and touches a live ball. For these rulings as well, bases are awarded per the umpire's judgment, and when any of the four interference types is called, the ball is ruled dead.

Obstruction. A fielder may not in any way impede the progress of a runner if he doesn't have possession of the ball or is not in the act of fielding the ball (either on the ground or on the receiving end after having being thrown the ball by another fielder). It is the umpire's decision as to what constitutes being "in the act of fielding the ball."

Someone once told me that when Oakland A's owner Charlie Finley would interview prospective play-by-play broadcasters for a job, one of the questions he would ask was, "What's the difference between obstruction and interference?" The answer: If a runner is stuck in a rundown between first and second, and the shortstop has the ball and is running him back toward first (the proper way to execute a rundown drill is to try to work the runner back toward the base he came from), and the runner runs into the second baseman—who is not part of the play—play is stopped and the runner is awarded second base, because the second baseman committed obstruction. If a runner at first is trying to steal second, and the catcher's arm—during an attempt to throw him out—hits the umpire standing behind him, that's umpire interference. And if Luis Castillo, of the Florida Marlins, hits a foul ball down the left-field line at Wrigley Field three rows deep that Cubs left fielder Moises Alou reaches into the stands to catch, and Steve Bartman prevents him from doing so, that's another Cubs tragedy in the making.

Overslide. When a player slides (or runs) into second or third base, he must maintain contact with the bag to stay safe. If I slid safely ahead of a play at third, beating the throw, but my momentum carried me off too far, I could be called out if the third baseman tagged me before I reconnected with the base.

Rundown. This is what happens when the defense has a runner caught between bases and attempts to get him out before he safely reaches either. One situation in which a rundown might take place is if, with a runner on second and one out, a batter hits a single that is played by the right fielder, who comes up throwing. As the runner rounds third and approaches home, with the ball in flight toward the plate, the catcher realizes that the throw will be too late to tag the runner out. Instead, he'll yell to his teammates to cut off the ball. The first baseman will catch the ball originally intended for the catcher. Frequently, the batter will be trapped somewhere between first and second base and eventually tagged out in a rundown. Note to second baseman: Do not cause interference!

Set Position. One of the two legal pitching positions.

Squeeze Play. A bunt with a runner on third is usually labeled a squeeze play, especially if the goal of the play is to score the runner. The first variation of this is the "safety squeeze," in which, with runners on first and third, the batter will bunt to try to stay out of a double play.

The best-known version of this play is the "suicide squeeze." Here, with fewer than two outs, a runner on third will break for the plate (as if he were stealing home) while the pitcher is in midmotion. The batter squares and bunts the ball to either first or third. When the suicide squeeze is done right, by the time the fielder gets to the ball, the runner has already scored. The risk is that the batter may miss the bunt, leaving the base runner to run into what will most likely be a sure out at home (hence the name).

Strike Zone. Officially, the strike zone is the area over home plate. Its high end is the midpoint between the top of a batter's shoulders and the top of his uniform pants (when he is prepared to swing), and its low point is the hollow beneath his kneecaps. Any ball pitched within the strike zone and not swung at is . . . wait for it . . . a strike.

The strike zone has changed eight times in 60 years. Fans think they know the strike zone because they see a superimposed box on TV. In point of fact, it is a negotiation, a box of air. Making things more difficult for the home viewer is the fact that most broadcasts record from center field, over the pitcher's shoulder, so the strike zone they think they're seeing is actually skewed by the camera angle.

Triple Play. If you've got this far and you already know what a double play is, you should be feeling confident about this one. A triple play is simply a play in which three offensive players are called out during an uninterrupted chain of events (provided there are no errors in between). So, with runners on first and second and nobody out, let's say the batter hits a line drive to the shortstop, and both runners make some advance toward the next base on contact. The moment the ball is caught, that's one out. But the runner at second has strayed off the bag, and the shortstop throws to the second baseman before the runner can return—two outs. The second baseman then hurries a throw to the first baseman, who is standing on the bag, and gets the ball there before the runner can get back to first. That's a triple play, and it's rare!

Waiver Trade. Everyone understands the basic concept of trading players, even if expectations are not always grounded in reality. Up until the trading deadline (about two months before the season ends), teams can swap players to either improve their chances for a postseason run or build for the future. The confusion creeps in after the deadline passes, when the only way to move a player is through waivers.

A waiver trade occurs either when or after a player is placed on waivers. The way it works is that a team publicly declares that a player is available. Other teams (in reverse order of the standings, first within the original team's same league, then the other league) each have an opportunity to claim that player. If no claims are submitted, the player has cleared waivers and is free to be traded anywhere.

When a waiver claim is made, one of three things can happen: (1) the team that put the player on waivers can pull him off the list, no longer making him available to trade; (2) the team can work out a trade and send the player to whatever team put in the claim; or (3) the team can let the player go and allow the other team have him (and, presumably, his large contract).

Sometimes teams will put a claim on a good player just to prevent their competitors from being able to go after him, but they do so at the risk of having his salary dumped on their payroll. This is how quality players clear waivers. A team will take a chance by putting a well-paid big name on the waiver wire, knowing that others will not risk the possibility of having to add to their payroll. They might also put a star on waivers to make another player (the one they're actually looking to trade) seem less valuable by comparison.

Wild Pitch. A pitch that is either too high or too low and cannot be handled by the catcher is ruled a wild pitch. A pitch that should be caught with ordinary effort but that gets away from the catcher nonetheless is ruled a passed ball. While the results are the same (and potentially disastrous with a runner on third), the former puts the blame on the pitcher's control, the latter on the catcher's defense (or lack thereof).

CHAPTER 2

Momentous Moments— from the Beginning Through World War II (1823–1945)

◆▬◆▬◆▬◆▬◆▬◆▬◆▬◆▬◆▬◆▬◆▬◆▬◆▬◆▬◆

Baseball is enveloped in its history more than any other sport. This book includes a compilation of that history, complete with a selection of unforgettable moments that, as you take up the game, you should know about. It is by no means the definitive history, but hard-core baseball fans are familiar with each stop on the list, and by reading what's to come, you'll know enough to not be utterly confused.

The Beginning

The earliest known reference to something called "baseball" can be traced to the mid-18th century, about 20 years before the Declaration of Independence. A diary kept by a man in Massachusetts was uncovered in 2008 that made a direct reference to the game.

While Cooperstown, New York, has long claimed to be the home of the birth of baseball, it makes a nice story but is now considered a myth. It appears pretty clear, though, that something called "base ball" was played on the East Side of Manhattan in 1823, probably near Park Avenue and 25th Street.

The New York Knickerbockers were a baseball team long before the Knicks were a basketball team in the NBA (or a poor imitation thereof, considering their record this decade) and were founded in September 1845. One of their members, Alexander Cartwright, wrote the rules for playing the game.

The following year, they played what is generally recognized as the first baseball game, in Hoboken, New Jersey.

In 1857, the first governing body of the sport was formed. The National Association of Base Ball Players comprised 16 clubs. It was called National even though all 16 clubs resided in the New York area. By 1867, however, it was actually national in scope, with more than four hundred clubs from coast to coast.

Even Civil War soldiers played baseball. Shortly after the war ended, players, for the first time, were paid for their services. The first team to pay players for their services was the Cincinnati Red Stockings, in 1869. To distinguish between professional and amateur players, the NABBP split into two divisions. The amateur division ceased to exist a few years thereafter, while the professional division became the bedrock for the first major league.

The National League of Professional Base Ball Clubs was born in 1876 to effectively replace the professional division of the NABBP. Only on its face was it professional in conduct. The new league was rife with player rebellion against the clause that regarded players as chattel of the ball clubs, with no rights of self-determination against teams no longer in championship contention (baseball's infamous "reserve clause" would keep players attached to the teams that signed them beyond the terms of their original contracts for another century). Also getting a rise from and casting a shadow against those 19th-century pioneers were player raids, forfeits, breached contracts, and, worst of all, rampant gambling.

Dozens of leagues came and went, such as the Union League in 1884 and the Players League in 1890.

The most formidable challenger to the National League was the American Association, founded in 1881. For several years, the AA actually met the National League in something resembling a World Series.

The NL, dominant and entrenched in major cities, had its first legitimate threat from the Western League, a rival league that was determined to gather the best players and build the most successful teams. Run by a man named Ban Johnson, it took the field in 1894. The Western League, originally operating in outposts such as Grand Rapids, Indianapolis, and Sioux City, soon relocated its clubs to larger cities and, in 1900, changed its name to the American League.

Under any name, all leagues adopted the reprehensible policy of segregation. A so-called gentleman's agreement forbade the use of African-American players. The ban was retroactive, as an unknown number of African-Americans were already playing baseball, some under the guise of being Native Americans or Hispanics. The color barrier remained in effect shamefully until 1947.

At a meeting in Chicago in September of 1901, the system of what would become the minor leagues was created with the formation of yet another National Association of Professional Baseball Leagues. Just as important, it established a World Series to be played between the National and American Leagues to begin play in 1903 (more on that in Chapter 11).

Dead Ball Era

The early days of baseball bear no resemblance to the modern game in relation to offense. Equipment was rudimentary and inconsistent, especially the implements of war—the bat and ball.

Scoring was the product of what we now call "small ball." Most hits were singles, with extra-base hits rare and home runs virtually nonexistent. Bunting and the hit-and-run were critical elements to success.

From the turn of the century until the one-man revolution named Babe Ruth, baseball was mired in what came to be called the "dead ball era."

During this period, pitching dominated, and four of the greatest pitchers ever established records that will never be broken. Cy Young was on his way to 511 wins. (EDitorial: Randy Johnson might be the last of the 300-game winners . . . ever.) Walter Johnson, Grover Cleveland Alexander, and Christy Mathewson dominated play as no other pitchers have in a century.

Babe Ruth Traded (1919)

Christmas came a day late for the Yankees in 1919. That was when they obtained Babe Ruth from Boston in a straight-cash transaction. It was made public January 3, 1920.

Why in the world would Red Sox owner Harry Frazee trade the pre-eminent two-way talent in the game? Ruth not only was single-handedly transforming the game with unprecedented power but also was proving to be an outstanding pitcher, having set a World Series record with 29 consecutive scoreless innings that would stand for 42 years. In what turned out to be his final season in Boston, Ruth batted .322 with a major-league record 29 homers and 114 runs batted in, his best year yet. He also threw 12 complete games.

If he were alive today, he would be Bill Gates, as he basically invented the home run and thereby revolutionized the game.

Nevertheless, Ruth was incorrigible and had tried Frazee's patience. He jumped the team on the final day of the 1919 season to play an exhibition game with another team whereby he would get paid on the side. He also wanted his salary, pegged at $10,000, doubled.

Frazee had traded big names in the past. In 1916, he moved his best player, Tris Speaker, a future Hall of Famer, to the Cleveland Indians.

After spurning a deal with the Chicago White Sox for Shoeless Joe Jackson and $60,000 in cash, Frazee sold Ruth to the Yankees for $100,000 and a loan of $300,000 to be used for the mortgage on Fenway Park.

With his having made blockbuster trades in the past as the Red Sox continued to dominate the decade of the teens, why would this one be any different?

Ruth had what might be described as a slow start in New York. Playing center field, he dropped a fly ball that cost the Yankees the ope≠ner and didn't hit a home run until the first of May.

When he got hot, though, Ruth was murder on pitchers in the American League. He batted .376 with 54 homers and 137 runs batted in.

Harry Frazee's Red Sox? They finished in last place in 1920 with 61 wins and 91 losses, 37 games out of first place. Frazee had a home in Boston, but his primary residence was on Park Avenue, and his great-grandson quoted him as once saying, "The best thing about Boston was the train ride home to New York."

With that said, the irony of Frazee's final resting place should come as no surprise. Babe Ruth is buried in Gate of Heaven cemetery, north of New York City. Harry Frazee lies in the adjacent cemetery, so they are joined in history eternally.

Babe's highest salary? $80,000.

Babe's Called Shot (1932)

There is no absolute, gold-plated historical account of what Babe Ruth did to Cubs pitcher Charlie Root in the third game of the 1932 World Series at Wrigley Field.

Here's what we do know:

Babe Ruth stepped out of the batter's box. He removed his cap and held up two fingers. He then *seems* to be pointing out toward center field. The Cubs are giving him the business from their dugout. Ruth then gestures again. Back in the batter's box, he swings and hits the ball into the center-field bleachers for a home run.

The legendary "called shot" is the biggest single component of the Babe Ruth mystique. We've been debating about it for almost 80 years.

One thing is sure: we really want to believe it.

In 1992, to commemorate the event's 60th anniversary, the Babe Ruth Museum in Baltimore conducted a survey asking if Babe called his shot. About 99 percent said they believed he did.

Former Cleveland Indians coach Johnny Goryl played for Root in the minor leagues in 1952 in Eau Claire, Wisconsin. He recalled that Root—who died in 1970—swore that Ruth didn't call it.

This much is also evident: There was no love lost between the two clubs. For one thing, new Yankees manager Joe McCarthy had been fired by the Cubs the year before. Further, Mark Koenig, the longtime Yankees shortstop, had been traded to Chicago in August. Although he hit .353 in 33 games, he was voted only a half of the postseason share of bonus money usually divided among teammates before the Series. That irritated some Yankees.

During batting practice before Game 3, Ruth and Lou Gehrig were putting on a display of power. At one point, Ruth supposedly yelled over at the Cubs dugout, "I'd play for half my salary if I could hit in this dump all the time!"

The Babe never confirmed nor denied he had called his shot.

He told a Chicago sportswriter, "I didn't exactly point to any spot, like the flagpole. Anyway, I didn't mean to. I just sorta waved at the whole fence, but that was foolish enough. All I wanted to do was give that thing a ride. Outta the park. Anywhere."

He continued, "I took two strikes and after each one, I held up my finger and said, 'That's one' and 'That's two.' That's when I waved to the fence. I just laughed to myself going around the bases and thinking, 'You lucky bum.'"

President Franklin D. Roosevelt was at the game. As Ruth rounded the bases, FDR leaned his head back and laughed loudly.

What is little known is that Ruth had answered the challenge. The previous inning, he missed a shoestring catch, allowing the tying run to score. (And don't we wish the "called shot" was true?)

Homer in the Gloamin' (1938)

The home run hit by the Cubs' Charles Leo "Gabby" Hartnett more than 70 years ago is legendary in Chicago.

On September 28, 1938, with darkness setting in and no lights in Wrigley Field to turn on, Hartnett, not only the catcher but also the team's manager since July 20, broke a 5–5 tie with a home run into the left-field stands at Wrigley Field for the victory that moved Chicago into first place. Three days later, the Cubs, having won 20 of their final 24 games, clinched the National League pennant.

Hartnett, the 1935 National League Most Valuable Player when he batted .344 with 91 runs batted in, was considered the best catcher in the National League in the years prior to World War II.

He was inducted into the Baseball Hall of Fame in 1955.

Lou Gehrig Bids Farewell (1939)

On June 2, 1925, New York Yankees first baseman Wally Pipp showed up to work with a headache, and the "Iron Horse" was born. Lou Gehrig replaced him and became the greatest first baseman ever. He and

Babe Ruth formed the most powerful combination in the history of the game.

Fourteen years later, he had played in 2,130 consecutive games, though there were a couple of close calls in 1933. In April, he was hit in the head by a pitch and was almost knocked unconscious—but he remained in the game! In June, he was ejected from a game but, having already batted, was given credit for an appearance.

Until his career was interrupted by the illness that ultimately would claim his life, he drove in nearly 2,000 runs (1,995) with almost 500 homers (493), a lifetime on-base percentage of .447, and a slugging percentage of .632. He was named to the first seven All-Star Games in history, won a pair of American League Most Valuable Player Awards, and took the Triple Crown in 1934.

Midway through the 1938 season, the Yankees' captain's skills began to mysteriously diminish. By the end of April the following season, he was batting .143 with a single RBI.

On May 2, 1939, prior to a game in Detroit, the Yanks' legendary first baseman took himself out of the starting lineup "for the good of the team" and was replaced by Babe Dahlgren.

One month later, on his birthday, June 19, Lou Gehrig was told by doctors after six days of testing at the Mayo Clinic that he had amyotrophic lateral sclerosis (ALS), a degenerative and incurable disease that attacks nerve cells in the brain and spinal cord, leading to weakness, paralysis, and eventually death. Two days later, the Yankees announced his retirement and their plans to celebrate a day in his honor.

On July 4, 1939, between games of a doubleheader, Lou Gehrig stepped to the microphone in Yankee Stadium. Delivered *without notes*, his "luckiest man" speech, which lasted just two minutes and seven seconds, prompted audible sobbing among the crowd of 61,808. The Yankees retired his uniform number 4, making him the first player ever to be accorded that honor.

On June 2, 1941, 16 years to the day after replacing Wally Pipp and 2 years after taking himself out of the lineup, Lou Gehrig died at age 38. (Moral of the story: *if you've got a headache, go to work anyway.*)

Ted Wins the All-Star Game (1941)

He called it the greatest hit of his storied career, and the guy got a *lot* of hits, ya know? Ted Williams was in his third year and on his way to a .406 season yet to be duplicated. At the time of the game, his average was a little off-mark.

.405.

Fellow all-star Joe DiMaggio had already hit in 48 consecutive games, en route to his record 56. The ninth All-Star Game took place July 8, 1941, at Briggs Stadium—later known as Tiger Stadium—in Detroit.

Eight future Hall of Famers represented the National League: Billy Herman, Carl Hubbell, Al Lopez, Joe Medwick, Johnny Mize, Mel Ott, Enos Slaughter, and Arky Vaughan.

Ten future Hall of Famers represented the American League: Luke Appling, Joe Cronin, Bill Dickey, Joe DiMaggio, Bobby Doerr, Bob Feller, Jimmie Foxx, Joe Gordon, Red Ruffing, and Ted Williams.

Feller started for the American League, which trailed 5–3 heading to the bottom of the ninth. Joe DiMaggio batted with the bases loaded and one out. He hit what appeared to be a certain game-ending double-play ball to short, but the relay throw from second baseman Billy Herman was wide, enabling DiMaggio to reach and a run to score.

If that throw had been good, one of the most glorified moments in All-Star Game history would never have happened.

Williams stepped to the plate. Earlier in the game, he had delivered an RBI double. With a 1 ball, 2 strike count, he sent a Claude Passeau fastball deep into the upper right-field stands for a 7–5 victory.

There is a film account of the home run in which Ted is seen skipping and clapping his hands in joy as he rounds the bases.

His manager, Del Baker, was so overjoyed that he hugged and kissed him in the locker room following the game.

Keltner Robs DiMaggio (1941)

Almost 70 years later, no one has come close to challenging Joe DiMaggio's record of getting a hit in 56 consecutive games.

Seventy years!

Ryan Zimmerman, of the Washington Nationals, got to 30 games early in the 2009 season before his streak was halted.

No one noticed.

Playing in Cleveland on July 17, 1941, Joe DiMaggio, the irresistible force, came up against Indians third baseman Ken Keltner, the immovable object.

Five years earlier, Keltner was driving a truck when he was discovered playing softball by the then minor-league Milwaukee Brewers. He became renowned as a superb fielder and was named to seven all-star teams over his 13-year career.

Not once, but twice, Joltin' Joe whistled hard-hit grounders toward third base that Keltner backhanded and turned into outs.

Phil Rizzuto told me that after the game ended, he was walking with DiMaggio on the streets of Cleveland. They came upon a bar, and Rizzuto turned along with Joe D to go inside.

DiMaggio stopped him from going in. He wanted to be alone.

Rizzuto never asked any questions and kept walking.

Purely Subjective List of the Greatest Hitters Since Ed's Been on Earth

Career batting averages are given, and active players (through the 2009 season) appear in **boldface**.

Ted Williams—.344

Tony Gwynn—.338

Albert Pujols—.334

Ichiro Suzuki—.333

Stan Musial—.331

Todd Helton, Wade Boggs—.328

Vladimir Guerrero—.321

Kirby Puckett—.318

Derek Jeter, Roberto Clemente—.317

Nomar Garciaparra, **Manny Ramirez**, Bill Dickey, Hank Greenberg, Larry Walker—.313

Magglio Ordonez, Edgar Martinez, Dale Mitchell, Johnny Mize—.312

Jackie Robinson—.311

Chipper Jones, Matty Alou, Don Mattingly, Mike Piazza—.307

Paul Molitor—.306

Hank Aaron, Ralph Garr, **Alex Rodriguez**—.305

George Brett, Bill Madlock, Tony Oliva—.304

Will Clark, Moises Alou, Mark Grace, Al Oliver—.303

Pete Rose—.302

Willie Mays—.301

CHAPTER 3
Batter Up— the Art of Hitting

◆◆◆◆◆◆◆◆◆◆◆◆◆◆◆◆◆◆◆◆◆◆◆◆◆◆◆◆◆◆◆◆◆◆◆◆◆◆

As a pitcher, what I looked to do when I came up to bat was to sit back down on the bench as soon as possible. See, I was scared of the ball. Soon after I had begun playing competitively in Little League, I was hit by a pitch. For the longest time, I was never able to overcome my fear of getting hit again.

I pretty much concluded my playing career (I *think* it was my choice) before the invention of the abomination known as the designated hitter. For the great ones, though, fear plays no role.

In 1897, Willie Keeler revealed his time-honored philosophy on hitting. After batting .432, he simply said, "Hit 'em where they ain't."

It sounds simple enough, and ultimately it makes sense.

Keeler's axiom, though, tends to ignore the obvious: How does one hit the ball to begin with? And how is it done with authority?

Ted Williams, the last player to hit .400, expended a lot of his postcareer energy explaining why hitting a baseball is about as hard as it gets in sports. "Nothing," Williams said in his book *The Science of Hitting*, "has as many variables and as few constants."

So, the first remarkable thing about these guys is that they can hit the ball at all. A batter has to judge the location and when the ball will be at a particular point at a particular time with incredible accuracy.

And he has to do it in a remarkably short period, about 0.4 second, against a very fast pitcher.

Batting Around Theories

From the 19th century until the 1980s, hitters were left to fend for themselves before hitting instructors were added to major-league coaching staffs.

What they teach differs, reflecting the variety of theories on just how to hit a baseball.

There is the head-down, release-the-top-hand style. There are the wait-and-react and attack-the-ball philosophies. All of the theories have their ardent followers and their share of successful laboratory mice to justify their claims.

What all the instructors agree on is that the hitter's body and bat should be in the best possible position when it is time for contact. It's what that position is, and how to get there, that can lead to arguments.

There is the popular notion that a hitter's stride should be completely separate from the swing itself. Take a short stride, keep the hands and weight back, and then decide whether to swing. Translation: in an activity that requires speed and quickness, be patient.

That's the opposite of aggressive movement to the ball, which dictates: decide to swing and then do it in one explosive motion.

Although the difference in the two theories may be undetectable in the blur of a swing, each side is vehement that its way is the best way. It all relates to timing and the fact that while so many pitches are thrown at different speeds, they all look strikingly familiar in the first two-tenths of a second after they are thrown. And it is in the first fractions of a second that a hitter has to decide whether to swing.

It is this problem of timing that has led more and more hitters to opt for a short stride as a counterattack.

The disadvantage of a long stride is that it needs to be started sooner, often before the speed of the pitch is apparent. That causes the body's weight to shift forward too quickly for slower pitches, and the power generated by the hips and the legs is released before the bat hits the ball. The results are weak ground balls or pop-ups.

Hall of Famer Paul Molitor took the short-stride concept to the extreme. In fact, he believes too many players come to the major leagues trying to pull the ball (hitting it to the same side of the field that they bat from), instead of waiting and using the whole field. Molitor had a stride that, over time, became infinitesimal. He gradually got rid of the movement, and doing so helped him take a longer look at the baseball.

Then again, Toronto hitting coach Gene Tenace, who was the bench coach when Molitor played there, considered him "a freak." According to Tenace, Molitor "used his hips, legs, and hands well." He noted, "That's difficult to teach, because he hit from a dead standstill. To generate bat speed, you need some movement backward, just like a golf swing. But he was successful, so you would never change that."

The question, though, is whether to change any player's swing at the major-league level. Most teams believe the best results come when a hitting coach works with the style of the particular hitter.

That's what made Steve Henderson so popular when he was the hitting coach with the Tampa Bay Rays, who went to the World Series in 2008. Carlos Pena, Tampa's first baseman, told me, "He just listens and doesn't fill your head with his theories. He doesn't complicate hitting. I don't overthink, and I can relax more."

Another Hall of Famer, George Brett, who batted .305 over 20 years in the majors, is proof, however, that substantial change can be beneficial.

"I worked with Charlie Lau for eight years," Brett said. "He changed my swing completely. I never hit .300 in the minors, but I hit .300 in the majors 12 or 13 times."

Brett concedes, though, that being only 20 when he fell under Lau's influence allowed him time to adjust. He doesn't recommend teaching the older dogs new tricks. Learning a swing, whether it is a batter's own or one that is being taught to him, is a tremendous investment in time.

A teammate of Brett's at Kansas City, Brian McRae, said, "It was at least nine years in pro ball before I started to understand what was going on."

It takes an inordinate amount of repetition and fine adjustments for a swing to become second nature for a batter.

As a Lau disciple, hitting instructor Walt Hriniak carried on the easy-to-spot tradition of keeping the head down, even after contact, and letting the top hand come off the bat.

The reason for keeping the head down is simple: if the head is lifted up too soon, the bat can change course, to the hitter's detriment. Detractors, such as Mike Easler, the Los Angeles Dodgers' hitting coach in 2008, argue that a head that stays down too long acts as a doorstop, preventing a good completion of the swing.

Then there's that top hand. Releasing it allows the bat to travel in the ball's path longer, as if there were a series of baseballs to hit, one behind the other. The effect is to compensate for any mistake the batter made in timing. Those who argue against it contend it robs the swing of power.

That claim raises the question of which hand provides the power. The bottom-handers believe the bat is pulled through the strike zone by the bottom hand. The top-handers, such as Ted Williams, maintain it is pushed through the zone with the top hand.

In the end, the arguments over the proper stride, over which hand is the power hand, and over how long the head should stay down are all secondary to a batter's properly seeing what he is swinging at.

What You See

Vision is a critical component in hitting. Most hitters are blessed with 20-20 vision or better. It was said that Babe Ruth could read a record label spinning at 78 rpm. Impressive, but keen vision in itself is only a basic prerequisite, one of as many as 30 visual skills that a good hitter needs.

Those other skills include the ability to make timing adjustments and to judge distances; excellent eye-to-hand and eye-to-foot reaction time; and concentration. There is also that old baseball basic known as dynamic acuity, which is how clearly you see motion, because vision may deteriorate when motion is introduced. And don't forget muscle memory, which conditions the body to react in a certain way to what it has seen. This adaptation is acquired through endless repetition.

With all of that, even good hitters lose out to the pitcher 7 out of 10 times. To boot, many pitchers add one more factor to the mix: fear.

With the ball traveling at such high speeds, and with the knowledge that it has broken bones and altered or ended careers, hitters can get leery. Don't think the pitchers don't know it. They also know that because of the exactness of a batter's swing, they will benefit if they can make the batter pause or flinch and thereby throw the swing out of kilter.

Even if a hitter does everything correctly, there are no guarantees.

In Game 7 of the 1962 World Series in San Francisco, future Hall of Famer Willie McCovey came to the plate with runners on second and third and two outs and with the Giants trailing pitcher Ralph Terry and the Yankees by a score of 1–0.

If McCovey gets a hit, the Giants win the World Series. If he makes an out, the Yankees do.

McCovey got a good look at a fastball and took a good swing. Hips, legs, and hands combined for a line drive that exploded off his bat—right into the glove of Bobby Richardson at second base.

The Giants lost.

In the 1993 World Series, Joe Carter, of Toronto, found himself in a similar situation, his team trailing by a run in the bottom of the ninth in Game 6, with runners on first and second and one out. Carter also got a good look at a fastball, from Mitch Williams, of the Phillies. A quick swing, and the ball burst off his bat and sailed over the wall. Series over. The Blue Jays win.

As Keeler said, hit 'em where they ain't.

Hitting a Baseball: So Much to Do, So Little Time

Hitting a baseball has often been called the hardest thing to do in sports, and considering that most hitters fail at least 7 out of 10 times, it probably is. Let's look at some of the mysteries of the batter's box and some of the methods that hitters use to solve them.

The Soft Focus

The batter watches the pitcher's windup with a soft-centered focus (as in a daydream). The eyes shift to the pitcher's release point at the last instance, and the lenses lock onto the ball.

Looking intently at the pitcher too soon will cause the eyes to become exhausted and lose focus. Some players refer to this problem as the trance.

Countdown to Contact

A batter has 0.4 second to interpret the best course of action in response to a released pitch:

The First 0.2 Second. The batter focuses on the pitcher's release point, while beginning the backward momentum of the swing. The rotation of the seams on the ball helps the batter determine the speed and ultimate location of the pitch. A decision must be made regarding when and where to swing.

The Final 0.2 Second. The final determination of pitch location is made by the hitter, who in most cases loses sight of the ball as it nears the plate. As the batter's weight is shifted forward and the hips turn, the hands throw the barrel of the bat through the path of the ball.

The Swing

During the same 0.4 second that a batter is deciding how best to attack a pitch (or not) he must also prepare his body for action:

Balance and Relaxation. Feet are spread at least shoulder-width apart, with weight evenly distributed on both legs. Hands hold the bat softly at the top of the strike zone. All muscles, including those of the eyes, are relaxed. (EDitorial: this would not be me.)

Stride. As the pitch is released, a short stride forward is taken, and weight is shifted to the back leg. The front shoulder turns inward, and the hands move back slowly.

. . . And Decide. When the speed and the location of the pitch have been judged, the decision whether or not to swing is made. If a batter decides to take a hack, his weight starts forward, hands remain back. The front leg stays slightly bent until contact.

Hands and Hips. Hands are thrown downward to the ball, creating the shortest path. The head follows the path of the ball. The back hip and shoulder are thrown toward the ball. Weight continues forward.

Lock and Explode. At contact, the front leg locks, while the back leg and hip explode toward the ball. (EDitorial: again, this would not be me. I never exploded toward the ball. Well, maybe once.)

The front arm is fully extended, and the back arm and the head remain behind the bat. The head is pointed toward contact.

Extend and Release. The bat continues along the path of the ball to correct the batter's error in timing. The head is released upward, allowing for a complete follow-through. Some players choose to release the top hand (per the Lau/Hriniak philosophy).

Choosing an Angle. Some players elect to keep the bat vertical for as long as possible through the swing. In this position, the bat appears lighter and the swing quicker. Although flattening the bat makes it feel heavier, some hitters do so. This position gets the bat on the plane of the ball earlier.

The Loose Grip. A loose grip yields a quicker swing, because the muscles aren't busy squeezing the bat. The grip becomes firm at contact.

Slow Feet, Quick Hands. Pitches are, of course, thrown at different speeds but look similar when a batter needs to decide whether to swing. This effect increases the problem of the batter's timing.

A short, slow stride allows the weight to shift backward while the batter steps forward. This breaks the inertia of the stance without committing the body to the pitch. The stride and the swing are separated, which helps increase timing.

Location, Location, Location

A batter's appraisal as to the trajectory of a pitched ball will affect his swing:

Outside Pitches. An outside pitch needs to be hit when the ball is closer to the plate, allowing the swing to remain compact.

Inside Pitches. An inside pitch should be hit well in front of the plate. The swing needs to start in time to get the hips open and the hands through.

Batter Up: What Hitters Look For

Indisputable fact: hitting is a guess.

Most hitters look for the fastball, the most dominant and frequent pitch in the game. Every pitcher has one. Not every one throws a curve, a slider, two-seam and four-seam fastballs, or a changeup.

Those odds favoring the fastball notwithstanding, it's a guess as to what's coming out of the pitcher's hand, isn't it?

In their ideal world, hitters are looking for a good pitch to hit—for "their" pitch. Then they decide whether to swing.

The most aggressive hitters are swinging unless they don't like the pitch or are under instructions to take a pitch.

There is a theory that in each at bat, a batter will get only one good pitch to hit. It is not universal. Several hitting coaches dispute the theory. They feel the quality of an at bat depends on the skill of the pitcher, who may inadvertently deliver more than one hittable pitch during the same at bat.

Regardless of approach, there's one constant: there is no substitute for bat speed.

The Physics of a Hit

Through the years, some major-league players have claimed that their bats actually bend when they hit home runs; that every bat has a single, particular "sweet spot"; and that heavier bats produce longer hits.

The last time you took a hearty cut at a baseball, if you heard a solid crack (or bong if your timber is aluminum) and watched the ball go glimmering on a long drive while your hands barely felt a kiss from the impact, congratulations. That was the sweet spot, that short stretch on the bat's barrel where, they say, hitting the baseball gives it the best ride—putting energy into the ball, not the batter.

If, instead, your hands stung like a fistful of bees, you definitely missed the sweet spot. If your top hand—the one farther from the knob—stung, then you caught the ball too close to the handle, and if the bottom hand stung, then you hit the ball too far out on the barrel.

It turns out that the bat, a simple-enough geometric shape, has not yielded all its secrets. While highly trained experts have some differences of opinion on how to make the perfect bat, some of what they *have* figured out may be a bit surprising. Most of it is just as useful to the weekend slow-pitch softballer swinging an aluminum bat (or one of the new graphite models) as it is to the major leaguer.

For instance:

- Most people use a bat that is too heavy. As a general rule, to hit the ball faster and farther, reach for a lighter stick. How much energy the ball gets is a function of both bat speed and bat weight. The typical batter is hurt more by the low speed of a heavy bat than he is helped by the modest gain in energy transferred by its higher mass. For the amateur player in your family, bats around 25 or 26 ounces may be best, lighter than almost anything now on the market and probably lighter than *can* be made of wood.

- It probably doesn't matter whether the bat is wood, aluminum, or graphite, everything else about the bat being equal. Compared with a baseball, all bats are so hard that their contribution to the ball's flight is about the same.

- There may be not just one but as many as three closely spaced yet still separate sweet spots on a bat.

- Hollow aluminum and other new-material bats are better than the wood variety because they allow for a light but wide bat. The sweet spot, therefore, can be made wider. In addition, of course, they don't break, which gives the batter a better shot at a bloop single off the handle.

A major-league bat must be solid wood of no more than 42 inches in length and no more than 2.75 inches in diameter. There are no weight limitations. Baseballs are 2.9 inches across, making this one of the few hit-the-ball sports in which the area of the striking implement is smaller than the ball.

Today's major-league batters have correctly figured out for themselves that a bat weighing from 32 to 34 ounces is about right. That has remained constant for generations. Shape, however, may be a different matter.

Bats have already changed enormously over the course of baseball history. Bats dating from more than a century ago bear little resemblance to contemporary models.

In the early days, a team might have had fewer than 10 bats altogether. If one broke, a nail and some glue would fix it. However, by the 1890s, special-made bats were the norm. Hillerich & Bradsby Co., of Louisville, Kentucky, maker of the Louisville Slugger brand, likes to call itself the originator of the modern bat. In 1884, the best hitter on the Louisville Eclipses splintered his bat. John "Bud" Hillerich, son of the owner of a wood-turning shop, made him a new one and thus launched the Louisville Slugger, with a shape much like that of the bats of today.

No firm date can be set, but the modern bat era might better be dated to around 1895, when a new rule was instituted requiring bats to be completely round. Before that, they could have flat spots.

As for the type of wood used, hickory bats were an early favorite. They were big and heavy and nearly unbreakable.

Now many wooden bats are made of northern white ash, trees that grow in Pennsylvania, the Adirondack Mountains of New York, and a few parts of Canada. It's the best combination of light weight and strength.

Bat makers will tell you the best wood comes from trees at least 45 years old, and there should be six to eight grains per inch. Any closer, the wood tends to be mushy; any wider, the wood is usually too heavy.

The straight, uniform grain needed for a professional-quality bat is not easy to find. It's estimated that of every one hundred "billets" of raw wood cut for bats, just one is good enough for the majors.

Babe Ruth is the best known of the founding stars of the game who swung a huge bat. Some people believe he started his career swinging a 54-ounce monster. In 1927, he hit his then record 60 homers using a 40-ounce bat, big by comparison with the 32-ounce bats of today.

Joe DiMaggio started out with a 42-ounce bat but cut down to 36 ounces later in his career. Fellow Hall of Famer Rogers Hornsby, perhaps the finest second baseman ever, used bats as heavy as 50 ounces.

Weight has been in a state of reduction. The 32- to 34-ounce bat that is typical now is 6 ounces lighter than the norm 20 years ago. Those changes in bat size have evolved mainly from instinct. Science has taken over since, with the development of aluminum and graphite bats.

The actual interaction of bat on ball takes only 1.2 to 1.5 thousandths of a second. In the blink of an eye, a batted ball has to be going around 110 miles per hour to make it over a fence. A 90-mile-per-hour fastball can contribute just 50 miles per hour to its outward path; to get out of the park, it has to pick up an additional 60-miles-per-hour's worth of energy from the bat.

It is not simple to measure or calculate how the batter puts energy into the bat. In the most basic theory, bat speed goes up as bat weight goes down. In other words, a light bat means a fast swing. However, one cannot assume a batter will put the same energy into two bats of different weights. Even with no bat at all in his hands, there is a limit to how fast a person can swing his arms. Below a certain weight, bat speed does not increase. The details depend on the batter's own physiology and physique.

Swinging a bat is not as easy as it seems.

Big Boppers I: Greatest Hitters for Power/500 Home Run Club

Alleged/Admitted to Have Used Performance-Enhancing Drugs

Career home runs are given, and active players (with numbers through the 2009 season) appear in **boldface**.

Barry Bonds—762

Sammy Sosa—609

Mark McGwire—583

Alex Rodriguez—583

Rafael Palmeiro—569

Manny Ramirez—546

Gary Sheffield—509

CHAPTER 4

Momentous Moments— the Golden Age of Baseball (1946–1957)

◆◆◆◆◆◆◆◆◆◆◆◆◆◆◆◆◆◆◆◆◆◆◆◆◆◆◆◆◆◆◆◆◆

World War II was over, and Bob Feller, who had volunteered for service two days after Pearl Harbor, along with Ted Williams, Joe DiMaggio, Hank Greenberg, and other baseball-playing soldiers returned to our shores to resume their careers.

The years 1946 to 1957 are often considered the golden years of baseball. Eight of the 16 major-league teams—half—made it to the World Series in that period. The Yankees were in the Series nine times, the Dodgers six, and no one else more than twice. The World Series got off to a rousing start in 1946, pitting two of the best hitters ever: Ted Williams, of the Boston Red Sox, against Stan Musial, of the St. Louis Cardinals.

The following spring, seven years before *Brown v. Board of Education* and before our military forces were desegregated, baseball's color barrier was shattered when Jackie Robinson became the first African-American to play professional baseball since the 1880s.

Called Shots
I have always maintained that, with all due respect to the eminent players that came before, baseball truly began in earnest when equality was realized on April 15, 1947, as Jackie Robinson took the field.

In the ensuing years, pennants flew in such uncharacteristic locales as Boston's Braves Field and Cleveland's Municipal Stadium (1948), not to mention Philadelphia's Shibe Park (1950). To manage their own star-studded team, the Yankees hired Casey Stengel, a failure as a manager with the Brooklyn Dodgers and Boston Braves, having notched one winning season in nine. In the Bronx, Stengel piloted the Yankees to five consecutive World Series championships from 1949 through 1953.

Joe DiMaggio bade farewell in 1951, but Willie, Mickey, and the Duke (Willie Mays, Mickey Mantle, and Duke Snider) fought for center-field supremacy in New York City, baseball heaven. At least one New York team played in the World Series every year but two from 1949 to 1964.

Suburban sprawl, air travel, the completion of the interstate highway system, and the advent of television helped alter the contour of the major-league map in the early '50s. After the 1953 season, the Boston Braves moved west to Milwaukee, while the St. Louis Browns headed east to become the Baltimore Orioles.

Though unsettling for many citizens, those moves would pale in comparison with the emotional trauma dispensed by the Brooklyn Dodgers and New York Giants, who moved to Los Angeles and San Francisco, respectively. New York, long a city of three teams, was down to one, with none in the National League. That remained the status quo for four years, until the National League expanded to 10 teams, adding the Mets and Houston Colt 45s.

The year before NL expansion, the American League led the way by expanding to the West Coast with the addition of the Los Angeles Angels, along with transforming the Washington Senators into the Minnesota Twins—replacing them in D.C. with . . . the Washington Senators. It didn't much matter, as the old saying still applied—Washington: first in war, first in peace, last in the American League. Expansion also made for a larger schedule, 162 games, up from 154.

Slaughter's Mad Dash (1946)

It remains one of the most daring baserunning plays in any World Series.

Playing the seventh game of the World Series at home in Sportsman's Park in St. Louis, the Cardinals led the Boston Red Sox 3–1 going to the eighth inning.

Dom DiMaggio tied the game with a hit but suffered a pulled hamstring, an injury that, many people believe, changed history.

Leon Culberson took over for him in center field before Enos Slaughter led off with a single. After the next two Cardinals were retired, Harry Walker came to the plate.

On a 2–1 count, the Cards put on the hit-and-run. As Slaughter broke for second, Walker struck a sharp line drive that dropped into left center field. Culberson got to the ball first, fumbled it momentarily, but quickly threw it to shortstop Johnny Pesky.

Slaughter, never breaking stride, ran through the stop sign of Cards third-base coach Mike Gonzalez.

What happened next is the subject of a debate that has been going on for more than 60 years.

Some people believe Pesky made the play he had to and was beaten by Slaughter's hustle. Others believe Pesky held the ball an instant too long and was so shocked to see Slaughter running with wild abandon around the bases that he made a weak throw to Sox catcher Roy Partee as the Cardinal scored.

St. Louis won the game and the Series 4–3. It was the most memorable play of Slaughter's career, immortalized with his induction into the Baseball Hall of Fame in 1985. The Cards retired his number 9 in 1996 and unveiled a statue at Busch Stadium depicting the Mad Dash three years later.

Jackie's Debut (1947)

Baseball pledged its allegiance on April 15, 1947, when Jackie Robinson left his wife and infant son at the McAlpin Hotel in Manhattan for his first day of work with the Brooklyn Dodgers.

He told his wife, Rachel, "I'll be number 42, just in case you have trouble picking me out."

Even though there was no locker for him waiting in the clubhouse, there was still a feeling of history in the air. On this day, baseball became the true national pastime when Jackie Robinson first set foot on a major-league baseball field. It remains the game's proudest and most powerful moment, a one-man freedom ride. As he crossed the foul line and made his way to his position, in the so-called noble experiment, he became a beacon of hope for everyone in our country in what was to become a monumental moment for baseball and civil rights. His first at bat could rightly be construed as the first step in the civil rights movement, coming seven years before *Brown v. Board of Education* and before our armed forces were desegregated.

The crowd count that afternoon at Ebbets Field was 25,623, more than 6,000 short of capacity. There were more African-American fans in the stands that day than ever before, perhaps accounting for as much as 60 percent of attendance.

It is not that Jackie Robinson integrated the field; it's that he integrated the stands.

It is fair to think that Brooklyn's teeming ethnic diversity made this city the only place anywhere that would have accepted Jackie. The newspaper writers behaved as if it were just another opening day at the ballpark, and, oh, by the way, a black guy is playing for the Dodgers.

There is a significant misconception in the notion that all Americans treated Jackie Robinson's debut as a historic day. They did not. Few people, black or white, initially appreciated how momentous the game was.

Jackie was the chosen one, selected by Dodger general manager Branch Rickey to carry the hopes of his race on his shoulders as much for his attitude as for his aptitude. He loved a fight. His chief assets were his tenacity and a knack for getting under an opponent's skin. One wonders how good he might have been without the burden of breaking the color barrier, though he was driven by the conviction that he had so much to prove.

There were nine mainstream daily newspapers in New York that day, and not one led its game story with Jackie. Perhaps baseball writers of that era didn't feel comfortable taking on such a big story.

The back page of the *New York Daily News* reported, "Dodgers top Braves 5–3; Yanks and Giants lose." The *Washington Post* devoted one paragraph to him, the *Pittsburgh Post-Gazette* two, the *Baltimore Sun* three.

The victory, played as history unfolded over two hours and 26 minutes, was the first of 94 Dodgers wins that season.

Jackie Robinson later admitted that he was nervous batting second. He went hitless not because of nerves, though, but because he was facing Johnny Sain. He was robbed once by the Braves' shortstop and another time by an umpire's call. Yet, he was said to look remarkably comfortable for someone at a new position, first base, as he handled 11 chances flawlessly.

He said after that first game that he was made to feel welcome by his teammates. Pitcher Ralph Branca said Jackie "was the best competitor I ever played with or against."

As the summer of 1947 wore on, it was said every kid in Brooklyn was imitating Jackie's pigeon-toed style of running.

He won the first-ever National League Rookie of the Year Award and passed on to you and me this moral tale: "A life is not important except for the impact it has on others."

The owners of the 15 other major-league teams had voted unanimously to oppose the integration of their game. Notwithstanding, in

Brooklyn, one man, Branch Rickey, carried for all of us the banner of decency, dignity, and fair play that is the American promise.

Rickey's victory was our victory.

Alone.

His defeat would have been our defeat.

Instead, Robinson batted .311 over a 10-year career, hit 30 or more doubles six times, led the National League in stolen bases twice, and had a .409 on-base percentage, a compilation good enough to earn his spot in Cooperstown in 1962.

To honor his memory, Jackie's number 42 is retired by every team in baseball in perpetuity. Every April 15, Jackie Robinson Day commemorates the man who carried baseball across the color line, with the entire country gradually to follow.

Until it was replaced in the summer of 2008, Jackie Robinson's Hall of Fame plaque made no mention of the fact that he was major-league baseball's first African-American player.

Al Gionfriddo's Moment in the Sun— Literally (1947)

Al Gionfriddo was hardly a household name in Brooklyn that season. Acquired by the Dodgers from Pittsburgh that May, the outfielder batted just .177 in 37 games.

He was fast, but at 5 feet 6 inches, he didn't scare anyone much.

Trailing three games to two, the Dodgers were fighting for their World Series lives in Game 6 before 74,065 fans in Yankee Stadium on October 5, 1947.

After starting Gene Hermanski in left field and replacing him with infielder Eddie Miksis, who had difficulty with one of the toughest sun fields in the game, Dodgers manager Burt Shotton went to Gionfriddo.

In the sixth inning with two out and two on and trailing 8–5, Joe DiMaggio, facing Joe Hatten, sent a long drive deep to left center field that was headed to the bullpen 415 feet away from home plate in a bid to tie the game.

Gionfriddo put his head down and ran, retreating to the fence, catching the ball over his shoulder in the webbing of his glove for the final out of the inning.

DiMaggio was almost at second base when Gionfriddo made one of the most fantastic catches in World Series history.

Not only is Gionfriddo immortalized for his catch, but also remembered is DiMaggio being caught on film kicking the dirt in frustration, a rare show of emotion for the Yankee Clipper.

Al Gionfriddo never played another major-league game.

The Shot Heard 'Round the World (1951)

Fifty years after the event, in 2001, it was declared by a vote of baseball fans still the most famous home run in the history of the sport.

After the Dodgers and New York Giants split the first two games of a three-game play-off to determine who would play the Yankees in the World Series, Brooklyn led 4–1 in the bottom of the ninth.

Playing at the Polo Grounds, the Giants scored a run to make it 4–2 and had two runners on base.

With the potential winning run at the plate, manager Chuck Dressen relieved starting pitcher Don Newcombe and replaced him with another regular starting pitcher, Ralph Branca.

The first batter was Bobby Thomson, who had homered off of Branca earlier in the play-offs.

After Thomson took a pitch for a ball, Branca threw a high fastball that Thomson tomahawked on a line into the lower left-field stands for a game-winning, three-run home run.

Still, rated the most famous in history.

Had It All the Way (1954)

Three years after Thomson's resounding shot, the same Polo Grounds became the setting for one of the greatest catches in World Series history, maybe the best ever.

In the opening game against the Cleveland Indians, the New York Giants were in a 2–2 tie in the top of the eighth inning. The Indians had two runners on base when left-handed pitcher Don Liddle faced the powerful Vic Wertz, who lifted a long fly ball to the deepest part of the ballpark in center field.

Willie Mays wheeled and turned, running full speed toward the wall, and miraculously caught the ball over his shoulder. More remarkable, he had the presence of mind to wheel and immediately throw the ball back to the infield.

The Giants went on to win that game and the next three, sweeping an Indians team that won 111 games during the regular season.

When New York manager Bill Rigney went out to the mound to make a pitching change, Liddle told his skipper, "Well, I got my man."

Safe at Home? (1955)

From now until forever, Yogi Berra will believe that he tagged out Jackie Robinson, who was coming off a subpar regular season in which he missed 49 games due to injury and batted only .256, with just 12 stolen bases.

In the opening game of the 1955 Subway World Series at Yankee Stadium, the Yankees led the Dodgers 6–4 in the eighth inning.

With Bill Kellert at bat, Jackie was on third and broke for home.

He is ruled safe by home-plate umpire Bill Summers. Yogi goes wild, jumping up and down in protest.

What is never discussed or recalled is that Yogi committed a rarely called catcher's balk. He had stepped out from the catcher's box to receive Whitey Ford's pitch before Kellert had a chance to swing at it.

No wonder Yogi had the plate perfectly blocked.

The play ultimately didn't matter. The Dodgers lost 6–5 as Ford beat Don Newcombe.

During his career, Jackie Robinson stole home 19 times.

And did not play in the seventh game as the Dodgers beat the Yankees for their only World Series victory over the Yanks in Brooklyn.

Beyond the Box Score

Every time Yogi Berra sees Rachel Robinson, he kisses her and tells her that her husband was out. Then he smiles.

Never Before, Not Since (1956)

Perhaps the most amazing aspect of Don Larsen's 2–0 perfect game in Game 5 of the 1956 World Series was that he didn't even know he was going to start until he got to Yankee Stadium.

By all accounts, it qualifies as a miracle. No one knows why it happened, or why an unlikely baseball player such as Larsen was the one who tossed it.

Just two years before, he led the league in losses as he won 3 and lost 21 for the newly minted Baltimore Orioles. Two of those wins came against the Yankees, who acquired him on November 18, 1954, in the first part of what would be an 18-player trade that would take two weeks to complete.

Usually, the Yankees would announce the starting pitcher the day before. On occasions in which the starter was not determined until later, legendary third-base coach Frank Crosetti would perform the ritual of placing a new baseball for that day's game in the starting pitcher's spike. And that's how Don Larsen found out he was pitching.

Who could blame the Yankees for being indecisive? A few days earlier, in Game 2, Larsen was wild, giving up four runs over not even two innings in a 13–8 loss.

On this day, in contrast, he used a dazzling array of blazing fastballs, darting sliders, and uncanny control to handcuff the mighty Dodgers. He threw just 97 pitches, only 26 of them balls, and five of his seven strikeouts were on called third strikes. Larsen said, "I never had control like that before or since."

Pitchers are supposed to be oblivious when they're throwing a no-hitter. Not Don Larsen. In the seventh inning, he came into the dugout, sat next to Mickey Mantle, and said out loud, "Wouldn't it be great if I pitched a no-hitter?" Mickey immediately moved away and yelled, "Shut up!"

Larsen then sneaked a cigarette.

After Dale Mitchell was called out on strikes to end the game (and incidentally, Babe Pinelli's career as an umpire), catcher Yogi Berra jumped into Larsen's arms, creating an iconic photograph etched in baseball fans' collective memory.

Believe it or not, it wasn't until after the game that Larsen learned of the full implications of what he had accomplished, when Yogi told him in the clubhouse that he had thrown not just a no-hitter but a perfect game.

Don Larsen could not remember a single day since in which the events of that afternoon in the Bronx did not come to mind (especially with a license plate summing it up succinctly: "DL 000"—no runs, no hits, no errors). For years, he told people that the beauty of his perfect game was that it is a record that can never be broken. "If you have to be remembered for one thing," he said, "that's a pretty good thing to be remembered for."

The *New York Daily News* headline said it all: The imperfect man pitched a perfect game.

Big Boppers II: Greatest Hitters for Power/500 Home Run Club

The Rest—Who Presumably Performed Unenhanced

Career home runs are given, and active players (with statistics through the 2009 season) appear in **boldface**.

Hank Aaron—755

Babe Ruth—714

Willie Mays—660

Ken Griffey Jr.—630

Harmon Killebrew—573

Reggie Jackson—563

Mike Schmidt—548

Mickey Mantle—536

Jimmie Foxx—534

Ted Williams, Willie McCovey, Frank Thomas—521

Ernie Banks, Eddie Mathews—512

Mel Ott—511

Eddie Murray—504

CHAPTER 5

The Art of Pitching— a Comprehensive Lesson (So, Heads Up)

◆◆◆◆◆◆◆◆◆◆◆◆◆◆◆◆◆◆◆◆◆◆◆◆◆◆

The size of pitching staffs has soared in the last decade, with every major-league team carrying 12 pitchers, sometimes 13, on its 25-man roster. Most teams carry five starters and seven relievers. The days of 9- and 10-man pitching staffs are over.

In 2000, 24 of the 30 teams had 11 or fewer pitchers on their opening-day rosters. In 2009, four teams opened for business with 11-man staffs. At one point, a trio of teams carried 13 pitchers: the Los Angeles Dodgers, Oakland Athletics, and St. Louis Cardinals. The Cleveland Indians even had a 14-man staff for a brief period.

Pitching has become specialized—critics would say perhaps too much so. Just look at the seven-man bullpen: you have one long man, to pitch when a starter is knocked out of a game early; two middle relievers, to be used between the fifth and seventh innings; two setup men, to pitch the seventh and eighth innings; a left-handed specialist; and a closer.

Expansion of pitching staffs has made it more difficult for managers to maneuver offensively, since fewer players are on the bench.

Mechanics

Mastering the mechanics of the fastball is one of the first steps to becoming a successful pitcher. Seemingly minor mechanical corrections and adjustments can increase velocity and control, as well as reduce the chance of injury.

Most professional pitching instructors subscribe to the "drop and drive" theory. Translation: get as low to the ground as possible, and drive directly toward the catcher's target, using the large muscles of the legs, hips, back, and shoulders to generate power, leverage, and momentum.

The Grip

Pitchers achieve movement on the fastball by using variations on the four-seam grip—that is, placing your fingers *across* the seams of the ball. The two-seam grip is *with* the seams. For either, the ball is gripped with the fingertips.

A changeup, also called in days gone by a palm ball or a slip pitch, is held farther back in the hand, resulting in less leverage and allowing the pitcher to throw a slower pitch without slowing his arm speed. It's important to keep the middle and index fingers together. They're stronger that way, yielding more velocity, control, and movement.

The position of the thumb is an often overlooked aspect of the grip. If the thumb is extended, the ball will tend to sink, because of the dragging effect. For more speed and movement, experts say, try tucking the thumb. The adjustment allows the ball to leave the hand with less drag.

Starting Position

The body should be upright or leaning slightly forward, never backward. One other tip: keep the chin over the belt buckle. If you start your windup by leaning back, you'll be in trouble, spending the rest of your windup trying to regain your balance, rather than generating maximum power toward the target.

It is also suggested that a pitcher not stand in the middle of the rubber. Generally, right-handers should pitch from the third-base side and left-handers from the first-base side. This increases the angles of trajectory, making it more difficult for a hitter to gauge where the ball is traveling. It also helps the pitcher step directly toward the target and avoid landing on the sides of holes that other pitchers have excavated.

A Rhythmic Delivery

The windup and delivery can be described as a four-step, rhythmic sequence. Each of the four sequential steps should be *on the beat* and of equal duration. You can learn to execute a rhythmic delivery by counting aloud or mentally: one-and-two-and-three-and-four.

One. The windup begins with a short step back (no more than 12 inches) on the non-pivot foot (left foot for righties, right foot for lefties).

And Two. Turn the pivot foot completely sideways in front of the rubber. If half the foot or some of the cleats are on top of the rubber, the body will tend to fall forward, rather than stay balanced and generate leg drive. That leads to *rushing*, which diminishes power and control.

And Three. Turn the body *completely* sideways to the target and raise the front leg, while bringing the hands together over the knee into a good balance position. Make a *full* turn of the hips and shoulders. *This is critical!* Full turn, hands together, balance.

And Four. Drop and drive, making sure the front foot steps directly on a line from the *heel of the pivot foot to the target*.

The Stretch

Working from the stretch, the pitcher omits both the short backward step with the non-pivot foot and the sideways turn of the pivot foot and instead begins with his pivot foot parallel to the rubber. From that point forward, the delivery from the stretch is identical to the delivery from the full windup.

Hand on Top

As the pitcher drops from his balance point and drives forward, he reaches back toward second base with his pitching hand. At this point, his throwing hand should be on top of the ball. Many pitchers are in the habit of having the hand on the side of the ball at the separation point (where they build torque). This causes them to have the hand on the side of the ball at the release point (where the ball is let loose), resulting in a soft slider type of pitch. If the hand is on top of the ball at separation, the hand will be behind the ball through the delivery and release, which increases speed and control.

Elevate the Elbow

Until the pitcher releases the ball, the elbow of the throwing arm should be at least as high as the shoulder. It's also important to keep the front shoulder closed as long as possible. With the front shoulder closed and the elbow elevated, the pitcher avoids overtaxing the muscles of the rotator cuff. And that's a *very* good thing.

Follow-Through

The wrist should remain loose and relaxed. Speed is also generated by extending the upper body and arm toward the target. The trunk rotates and bends over simultaneously, creating thrust and torque over two axes. The follow-through should be a natural completion of a healthy delivery, with the throwing hand passing below the opposite knee.

When the pivot foot ends up a few inches closer to the target than the stride foot, and the body is low and on balance, with the back flat (parallel to the ground), you've pushed off properly, and your mechanics are correct.

One Thing at a Time

It all works together. Work on one component at a time: getting your rhythm, making a full turn, balance point, fingers together, elbow higher than the shoulder, getting as low as possible, stepping directly toward the target, and extending the upper body. With each improvement, you should be able to make more quality pitches with more power and control, and with less discomfort.

Someone who improves five components of the delivery by 1 percent can go from 75 mph to 79 mph, or from 80 to 85. During an average 100-pitch game, a pitcher's ratio of strikes to balls could go from 60/40 to 65/35. It really makes a difference.

Recommended Drills

Whether you're taking the mound yourself or watching your favorite team warm up prior to a game, here are some more common drills for pitchers:

Long Toss. After warming up, throw with an arc trajectory from 90 feet, and then from 120 feet, and then from 150 feet or more, gradually increasing the distance.

Sit-Ups. Stomach strength is a good indicator of general body strength. Being able to pull forward and down with abdominal muscles is very helpful in the follow-through.

Stretching. Proper stretching prevents injuries, and increased flexibility can add speed and endurance.

Balance Point. Practice balancing on the pivot foot for up to five minutes. This drill strengthens the ankle muscles and balancing mechanism.

Running and Conditioning. Pitchers need stamina. Aerobic exercises build stamina. Find what works best for you.

Pickups. For each participant, place a straight line of balls spaced about 10 feet apart from each other. Starting from an infielder's crouch, execute a crossover step to the right, run five or six steps, squat to pick up a ball (without bending over from the waist), execute a crossover step to the left, run five or six steps, squat to pick up a ball. *This is murder.* Go easy at first.

When I used to do pickups, during the period in which the earth's crust was still cooling, my teammates and I used to do sets of 25 or 50. All I can say is that afterward, your legs feel exhilarated. You can't breathe, but your legs feel exhilarated.

Grip Strengthening. Squeeze something, such as a Silly Putty–type squeeze ball.

Word of warning: Before a player attempts to put any of these techniques and principles into practice, or undertake the suggested exercise program, the player's general physical condition should be assessed—with specific attention paid to the flexibility and soundness of the legs, back and spine, shoulders, and arms. A personal physician is usually best qualified to make such assessments.

A Game of Inches

Baseball is a game of energy, angles, and degrees as well as of inches. The laws of physics govern baseball as surely as its official rule book does. Here is a look at some of the little-known factors that affect the game.

The Equipment

A brief lesson on two-thirds of the holy trinity of baseball gear (gloves being the final piece of the puzzle):

The Ball. Major-league baseballs are 9 to 9.25 inches in circumference and weigh between 5 and 5.25 ounces. They have a small core wound with 316 yards of three different kinds of yarn. That is covered with two pieces of cowhide held together with 216 raised red cotton stitches.

The Bat. Major-league bats are made of ash. Almost all are shorter than 36 inches and weigh between 31 and 36 ounces. The barrel can be 2.75 inches in diameter, but many of today's bats are 2.5 inches in diameter to save weight. The ideal point of contact on a bat is known as a node and is the point where maximum energy is transferred to the ball. It's also one of the "sweet spots" mentioned in Chapter 3. Balls that are hit at the antinodes do not travel as far because much of the energy transferred is lost as vibration.

Ball-Bat Interaction

The bat and ball are in contact for about 0.001 second. Here is the skinny on what happens:

- A force of 8,000 pounds is required to change the direction of a 90 mph pitch to a 110 mph hit that will travel 400 feet.
- The ball is compressed to about one-half its diameter.

- The bat compresses about one-fiftieth as much as the ball.

- Most of the energy in the ball and bat is lost as heat.

- The baseball returns about 35 percent of the energy it receives during compression. It is this energy return that causes the ball to rebound from the bat.

- There are two factors that determine the distance a batted ball will travel: the speed at which the ball is pitched and the speed with which the batter hits it.

Dynamics of a Pitched Ball

The stitching on a baseball makes the ball travel through the air faster than it would if it were smooth. This is because the stitches create turbulence, which forms a boundary layer near the surface of the ball and thus reduces air friction. Here is an example using a fastball:

	Initial velocity	Velocity at plate
Smooth ball	100 mph	83 mph
Ball with stitches	100 mph	90 mph

A pitched ball can rotate as fast as 1,800 rpm. Because only 60 feet 6 inches separate the pitcher's mound from home plate, that means a 70 mph pitch would rotate about 15 times. Spin, or lack of it, is responsible for how pitches behave.

Pitching Trajectories

A fastball with an initial velocity of 98 mph will fall 3 feet on its way to the plate because of gravity. Backspin of 1,200 rpm will cause the ball to rise about 4 inches, making the drop 2 feet 8 inches. The ball will cross the plate in 0.4 second at 90 mph, having slowed about 1 mph for each 7 feet of travel.

Why a Curveball Curves

Curves curve because of aerodynamics and air resistance. It's much the same with sliders, knuckleballs, and all other pitches that are not fastballs. The faster-flowing air under the ball creates less pressure, which forces the ball to dive or break. The "curve" takes place when the stitching on a spinning ball gathers up air while it rotates, creating higher air pressure. The pressure makes the air on one side move faster than on the other. When air pressure is greater on the third-base side than the first-base side, the ball will move along a gradual curve toward first base, and vice versa.

From the point of view of a batter standing at home plate, curveballs seem to break—that is, move suddenly in a new direction. Scientists have calculated that the typical curveball goes through only approximately 3.5 inches of deviation from a straight line drawn between the pitcher's hand and the catcher's glove. However, from the batter's perspective, the break is exaggerated. That's because curves do most of their work as they near the batter. If a ball curves 14 inches after leaving the pitcher's hand, half of that deflection occurs in the last 15 feet. Not only that, but also, keeping in mind what was said about pitching trajectories and speed, if a ball was thrown with an initial velocity of 70 mph, it crosses the plate in 0.6 second but is traveling at a diminished speed of 61 mph. As you can see, what with the changes in trajectory, direction, and speed, a batter must adjust to a lot in what amounts to only a little more than half a second.

As a right-handed pitcher with a roundhouse curve (thrown from a ¾ overhand position), I would throw that pitch over and over again. It was my best weapon, and I could throw it consistently for strikes in the fervent hope that I didn't hang one that would be hit to the moon. I would grasp the ball with my index and middle fingers held together. As I released the ball, I would snap my wrist inward, as if I were turning the knob on a door. The ball would spin in the direction of the throw. If the batter was right-handed, and almost all were, I would start the pitch at his left shoulder. Some batters would actually bail out, fearing that the ball would hit them.

As a result of my throwing that roundhouse curve over and over beginning at age 12, by the time I reached age 18, my elbow was killing me. Although sympathies in the form of cash and checks to your favorite charities are always appreciated, the true moral here is to be aware that young arms are not physiologically ready for the traumas that throwing a curve will inflict on them.

The Environment

Environmental factors govern the distance a fly ball will travel. The examples that follow assume a ball has been hit properly and with enough energy to propel it 400 feet.

Altitude. The higher the stadium, the thinner the air, and the farther the ball will travel:

City	Altitude (in feet)	Distance ball will travel (in feet)
Miami	10	400
New York	55	401
Toronto	300	402
Los Angeles	340	402
Chicago	600	405
Kansas City	750	406
Minneapolis	815	406
Atlanta	1,050	408
Denver	5,280	440

Wind. A 10 mph wind makes a difference of about 30 feet:

Wind speed	Distance (in feet)
10 mph toward batter	370
No wind	400
10 mph away from the batter	430

Temperature. The warmer the temperature, the farther the ball will travel:

Degrees F	Distance (in feet)
45	400
55	404
65	408
75	412
85	416
95	420

Other Factors

Some other factors that affect the game include:

- A one-inch reduction in the barometric pressure adds about 6 feet to the flight of a 400-foot fly ball.

- Humidity makes little difference. Balls absorb moisture, becoming heavier and traveling shorter distances, but balls carry farther through moist air, so the two factors cancel each other out.

Nolan Ryan

In the 6,022 games that the New York Mets, a pitching-oriented organization, have played since trading Ryan, through the 2009 season (along with the 1,622 they played prior to the trade), they have never had a no-hitter. Nolan Ryan, who started 773 games in his career, pitched seven no-hitters.

Let us count the ways:

#1: May 15, 1973—California at Kansas City

Final score: Angels 3, Royals 0

Ryan's line: 9-0-0-0-3-12 (innings pitched-hits-runs-earned runs-walks-strikeouts)

Saving play: Angels shortstop Rudy Meoli raced into short center field to catch Gail Hopkins's soft line drive for the final out of the eighth inning.

Game notes: Kansas City manager Jack McKeon played the game under protest after complaining that Ryan was not keeping his foot in contact with the pitching rubber. Jim Evans, the plate umpire, had warned Ryan in the early innings about getting a walking start.

#2: July 15, 1973—California at Detroit

Final score: Angels 6, Tigers 0

Ryan's line: 9-0-0-0-4-17

Saving play: It's Rudy Meoli to the rescue again. The Angels shortstop saved the no-hitter when he made a leaping catch of Gates Brown's line drive with one out in the ninth.

Game notes: Longtime Detroit first baseman Norm Cash brings a furniture leg to the plate, but umpire Ron Luciano makes him use a bat. Ryan joins Johnny Vander Meer, of Cincinnati; Allie Reynolds, of the Yankees; and Virgil Trucks, of the Tigers, as the only pitchers with two no-hitters in a season.

#3: September 28, 1974—Minnesota at California

Final score: Angels 4, Twins 0

Ryan's line: 9-0-0-0-8-15

Saving play: The closest the Twins got to getting a hit comprised a pair of long fly balls to left by Glenn Borgmann, both snared by John Balaz with over-the-shoulder catches.

Game notes: Ryan becomes the sixth pitcher with three career no-hitters. The other five were Sandy Koufax (four), Bob Feller, Jim Maloney, Larry Corcoran, and Cy Young.

#4: June 1, 1975—Baltimore at California

Final score: Angels 1, Orioles 0

Ryan's line: 9-0-0-0-4-9

Saving play: In the seventh inning, Baltimore pinch hitter Tommy Davis led off with a high bouncer over the mound. Second baseman Jerry Remy raced to his right, gloved the ball, and barely got Davis, a slow runner, at first.

Game notes: Ryan ties Sandy Koufax's record with his fourth no-hitter. The victory is the 100th of his career. The last time Ryan had faced the Orioles, on May 18, he held them hitless until the eighth.

#5: September 26, 1981—Los Angeles at Houston

Final score: Astros 5, Dodgers 0

Ryan's line: 9-0-0-0-3-11

Saving play: His closest call came in the seventh when Mike Scioscia hit a deep drive to right center. Terry Puhl, the Houston right fielder, made the catch on the run just steps from the warning track.

Game notes: Ryan becomes the first pitcher with five no-hitters. The final pitch was a high curve, but Dusty Baker, looking for a fastball, got too far out front and hit the ball on the ground.

#6: June 11, 1990—Texas at Oakland

Final score: Rangers 5, A's 0

Ryan's line: 9-0-0-0-2-14

Saving play: None—the Athletics never came close to getting a hit. Willie Randolph fouled out to end the game.

Game notes: Ryan becomes the oldest pitcher, at 43, to throw a no-hitter and the only pitcher to throw one for three teams. His back hurt so much that he had an appointment scheduled with a specialist the next day. In his previous five starts, he was 0–3 with an 8.86 ERA.

#7: May 1, 1991—Toronto at Texas

Final score: Rangers 3, Blue Jays 0

Ryan's line: 9-0-0-0-2-16

Saving play: The closest the Blue Jays came to a hit was in the sixth when Manny Lee hit a blooper, which was caught on the run by Gary Pettis at his shoe tops.

Game notes: The Blue Jays were leading the majors with a .276 team batting average. Roberto Alomar struck out for the final out. His father, Sandy, was the Angels' second baseman during Ryan's first two no-hitters in 1973.

I was in love with Nolan Ryan from the moment I got my first glimpse of him in the big leagues with the New York Mets on September 11, 1966. His fastball was breathtaking. He was exasperating in his early years, inconsistent from start to start, but when he was on, it was a thing of beauty. So, in December 1971, I report for duty at my college radio station, WFUV, on the campus of Fordham University. It is the week of the baseball winter meetings. The old Teletype wire machine from the Associated Press has just reported that Ryan was the key player in a five-player deal with the California Angels. I ask one of my classmates, "Who were the four players the Mets got?" I'm told, "No, no, no. The Mets traded Ryan and three other guys for Jim Fregosi." *What?* Ryan was 29–35 for the Mets, who also had Tom Seaver and Jerry Koosman. They must have figured that was enough. Fregosi, a lifelong shortstop, was imported as yet the latest in a long list of infielders acquired to plug the club's eternal weakness at third base. Even Fregosi admitted years later he never would have traded Ryan for him. In 1972, Fregosi batted .232; Ryan won 19 games, pitched nine shutouts, struck out 329, and had a 2.28 ERA. Whether or not Fregosi was a bust—and he'll be the first to tell you he was—it remains the worst trade in Mets history, worse even than the Seaver trade in 1977. At least they received serviceable players in return for Tom. Fregosi, whose average had climbed to .234 in the first half of the following season, got sold to Texas on July 11, 1973. Ryan would strike out 1,176 different players over the course of his career.

Nolan Ryan holds the records for most career strikeouts (5,714), most strikeouts in a season (383 in 1973 with the Angels), and most no-hitters (seven). He threw his final no-hitter at age 44. He also shares with Bob Feller the major-league record for most career one-hitters (12). He spent 27 seasons in the big leagues, finishing with a 324–292 record and a 3.19 ERA. His 61 shutouts rank seventh all-time, and he's tied for 14th on the all-time win list. He led the league in strikeouts 11 times, in ERA twice, and in shutouts three times and was a 20-game winner twice. He ranks second in all-time career starts.

See? Really, really, really bad deal!

Purely Subjective List of the Greatest Starting Pitchers Since Ed's Been on Earth

Career number of wins are given, and active players appear in **boldface**.

Sandy Koufax—165

Bob Gibson—251

Warren Spahn—363

Greg Maddux—355

Roger Clemens*—354

Steve Carlton—329

Nolan Ryan, Don Sutton—324

Phil Niekro—318

Gaylord Perry—314

Tom Seaver—311

Tom Glavine—305

Randy Johnson—300

Early Wynn—300

Tommy John—288

Bert Blyleven—287

Robin Roberts—286

Ferguson Jenkins—284

Jim Kaat—283

Jim Palmer—268

Jack Morris—254

Juan Marichal—243

Whitey Ford—236

Luis Tiant—226

Catfish Hunter—224

Pedro Martinez—214

Roy Halladay—139 (one of the best starting pitchers
in baseball in 2009)

Why are Koufax and Gibson on top of my list even though they
have fewer career wins? Because I said so. Ask the same question
as to why there's an asterisk (*) next to Roger Clemens's name,
you'll get the same answer.

Special Mention

John Smoltz—210 wins, 154 saves—whose unselfishness in his
22-year service with the Atlanta Braves spawned two successful
careers born from the club's needs. He is going to the Hall of Fame
anyway.

CHAPTER 6
Momentous Moments— Expansion (1958–1967)

Once upon a time, there were two teams apiece—one in each league— in the cities of St. Louis, New York, Philadelphia, and Boston (New York actually could boast three: the Yankees in the American League, and the Giants and Brooklyn Dodgers in the National).

Until the late 1950s, the westernmost outpost of Major League Baseball was St. Louis, with its Cardinals in the National League and Browns in the American. The Browns left after the 1953 season and relocated east to become the Baltimore Orioles.

After the 1957 season, the Dodgers and Giants made a seismic shift from New York that opened the West Coast far beyond the banks of the Mississippi River.

In Philadelphia, where it was once the Phillies in the National and the Athletics in the American, the A's moved to Kansas City in time for the 1955 season; they then moved again and began 1968 as the Oakland A's.

Boston had the Braves in the National League and the Red Sox in the American. After the 1953 season, the Braves packed up and moved to Milwaukee. They would win the 1957 World Series over the Yankees and go on to lose the Fall Classic to them in the seventh and final game the following October.

They called in the movers again after the 1965 season and became the first team in the Deep South as the Atlanta Braves.

As the other three major sports leagues shifted franchises with more frequency through the decades, Major League Baseball was justifiably proud that its teams remained stable for approximately 40 years, an extraordinary length of time.

That stability ended in the winter of 2004 when the Montreal Expos became the third franchise to call our nation's capital home, as the Washington Nationals. The Nats stepped into the breach long since established by the escape of the Washington Senators and their forebears, the Washington Senators.

The original Senators moved to the upper Midwest to become the Minnesota Twins in 1961. The American League subsequently expanded back into Washington with another team called the Washington Senators. They lasted until 1971, when they moved to become the Texas Rangers. Until the Nationals arrived, baseball was vacant in D.C. for 35 seasons.

The Continental League

In a universe long ago and far, far away, the Supreme Court of the United States declared that Major League Baseball was exempt from the antitrust laws of the land, ruling that it was not engaged in interstate commerce. (*How* this is possible I have no idea.)

Cities that lost clubs were, in some cases, apathetic and in others, such as New York, apoplectic. One New Yorker, an attorney named Bill Shea, decided to do something about it. Shea announced the formation of the Continental League in the belief that the Sherman Antitrust Act was a restraint-of-trade violation to be challenged and, ultimately, overturned.

Originally, Shea was the leader of a New York committee whose goal was to acquire another major-league team for the city after the departure of the Dodgers and Giants. When attempts to attract an existing team failed and expansion seemed delayed, Shea chose to go the Continental route.

The Continental League won immediate credibility—and gained unmatched knowledge, insight, and experience—by naming the legendary Branch Rickey, responsible for breaking baseball's color barrier with the signing of Jackie Robinson for the Brooklyn Dodgers, as its president. Its original member cities were New York, Toronto, Houston, Minneapolis–St. Paul, and Denver, with Atlanta, Dallas–Fort Worth, and Buffalo warming up in the bullpen to join at a later time.

Once its teams were established, the Continental League received a scare from the majors. With Rickey in the midst of negotiations with the AL and NL to further the Continental's cause, they each announced their intentions to expand into new markets. The AL was talking with Minneapolis–St. Paul, and it proposed a plan that would include a New York team in the NL, to form two nine-team leagues. That would have established interleague play long before it became a reality in 1997. In December 1959, though, National League president Warren Giles said his league was rejecting the notion to expand because it lacked "sufficient sentiment" to do so.

Even with the NL and AL unable to agree on expansion, the Continental struggled with—and got hopelessly mired in—the territorial and indemnity problems that would have been created by its teams. After attending a meeting without further progress on those volatile issues, proponents of the Continental League abruptly threw in the towel on August 2, 1960, with the league's having never played a game.

About two months later, the NL did an about-face from its earlier stance and voted unanimously to expand in 1962, adding New York (Mets) and Houston (Colt 45s). Within days, the AL decided to expand to 10 members "no later than December 1, 1960," and it soon awarded teams to Los Angeles and Washington (which was losing the Senators to the Twin Cities). Suddenly, the 16-team major-league structure, in place since 1901, would grow to 18 and then 20 teams.

Amazing as it seems, baseball had made a major decision—to expand—and seen it through only months before the start of a new season, with the Los Angeles Angels and the new and perhaps improved version of the Washington Senators beginning play in April 1961. Nowadays, it would take a miracle for such quick action. Witness the move of the Montreal Expos, which were seized by the National League before the 2002 season and moved three years later.

No, the Continental League never got on the field, and yes, the majors surely would have expanded on their own in due time. Nevertheless, the specter of the Continental League surely forced expansion before owners really wanted it.

No Curtain Call (1960)

Even as the Boston Red Sox went into a free fall in the '50s, Ted Williams continued to provide brilliant theater, batting .388 in 1957, including .403 at Fenway Park. He was 39 at the time, the oldest player ever to win a batting title.

This is the Ted Williams whose eyesight was measured as 20-10 the year after he batted .406. More than 60 years later, no one has hit .400.

Williams lost nearly five years of his career to two wars—as a Marine Corps pilot in World War II as well as Korea—where he flew a combined 39 combat missions, was shot down twice, and had John Glenn as his wingman, who called him the greatest pilot he ever saw. And Glenn was good enough to qualify as one of this country's original seven Mercury astronauts!

It was not a state secret that Ted Williams had a contentious relationship with the local media in Boston. In fact, he could make *writer* sound like a four-letter word.

Slowed by a pinched nerve in his neck, he batted .254 in 1959. Team owner Tom Yawkey suggested he retire. Instead, he came back for one more year after voluntarily taking a 30 percent pay cut, from $125,000 to $90,000.

On an overcast day, September 28, 1960, Ted Williams bade his Fenway fans farewell.

Facing Baltimore's Jack Fisher in his final at bat in the eighth inning, Williams drove a 1–1 pitch to center field. It landed where the bullpen met the wall and disappeared, the 521st home run of his career.

Williams rounded the bases quickly, head down, unsmiling, refusing to tip his cap. The crowd chanted, "We want Ted!" for several minutes.

But there would be no curtain call, no recognition of his immortality, despite teammates and even umpires begging him to respond.

The man who made an argument for recognition as baseball's most accomplished hitter was a target of the Yankees, who wanted to sign him in 1961 strictly as a pinch hitter. Detroit asked him to manage. Instead, he spent nine years in retirement before returning to the game as the manager of the expansion Washington Senators. Williams took home Manager of the Year honors in 1969, and he stayed with the club through their relocation to Texas (as the Rangers) before retiring again in 1972.

His standard of performance was without peer. That standard was sustained by an unquenchable hunger to be the best. Ted Williams's goal was simple. He wanted people to look at him and say, even as an old man, "There goes Ted Williams, the greatest hitter who ever lived."

He was.

No Rebound (1960)

One swing. One big swing. One swing for the ages.

How many players can say they even came within shouting distance of something remotely resembling that? William Stanley Mazeroski could.

To say he came from humble beginnings would be an understatement. Growing up in the coal country of southeastern Ohio in a tiny town called Rush Run, in a little wooden house with no electricity or running water, where the sun lit his days and kerosene his nights, he would often hit stones with a broomstick by himself, using markers to determine whether his hits were singles, doubles, triples, or home runs.

He imagined a hundred times, maybe a thousand, that he was like Babe Ruth and that one of his home runs would come in a World Series.

Then he got to do it for real.

His immortal blast at 3:36 P.M. eastern time on October 13, 1960, barely cleared the left-field wall 406 feet away at old Forbes Field. It gave Pittsburgh a 10–9 victory over the heavily favored Yankees, who scored more runs (55 to 27), had more hits (91 to 60), hit more homers (10 to 4), and had a higher average (.338 to .256) in the Series.

The Yankees' three wins were by scores of 16–3, 10–0, and 12–0.

It remains the only walk-off home run in history to end a seven-game World Series.

Yogi Berra was playing left field that day for the Yankees when Mazeroski hit the ball off Ralph Terry. He told me he ran back and turned around to face the wall, expecting a rebound. Instead, the ball sailed over the top, scraping the vines on the way down.

On the plane home to New York, Yogi said he saw something that he had never seen before: Mickey Mantle crying inconsolably, in the belief that the wrong team had won.

Blame Bill Mazeroski, who later admitted that the Yankees were the better team that 1960 season. His first thought upon reaching second base and seeing left-field umpire Stan Landes signal home run was, "We beat the Yankees, we beat the mighty Yankees!"

The memory is rekindled by Pirates fans who still cherish that joyful moment and gather to celebrate it every October 13 at 3:36 P.M. at the spot where the ball landed, perhaps because of who the opposing team was and perhaps because it gave the city of Pittsburgh its first championship since the 1925 World Series.

During the game, the drama had been so intense that Bill Mazeroski didn't even realize, initially, that he was the leadoff batter in the bottom of the ninth. When he stepped into the batter's box against Terry, he was thinking, "Get on base."

After a first pitch that was high for a ball, Maz said, Terry's next delivery looked like a fastball. But it was a slider. Terry couldn't get it down in the strike zone.

Mazeroski, guessing on the pitch, looked for the only pitch he could hit for distance—as he called it, "swinging for the pump."

As with Don Larsen and his perfect game, Bill Mazeroski said he talks to someone about his heroics nearly every day. At the time, he figured it was a home run to win a ball game and it would be over with. But all these years later, it lives on, the memory an instant cure for whatever might ail anyone—in towns large and small all over western Pennsylvania.

In Pittsburgh, he will forever be Maz-nificent.

Roger Maris Against the World (1961)

Babe Ruth, the iconic "Sultan of Swat," hit 60 homers in 1927. The record would stand for 34 years. Roger Maris's would last two years longer, 36, ending in 1998.

No one wanted Roger Maris or anyone else to ever break the record. That included the commissioner of baseball himself, Ford Frick, who once covered Ruth as a newspaperman in his younger days. Other writers dismissed Maris as unworthy of wearing Babe's crown.

It took its toll.

Many years later, Maris admitted, "I often wonder what my baseball career would have been had I not hit the 61."

But Maris, whose left-handed swing was tailored perfectly for the short right-field fence at Yankee Stadium, mounted his assault through the summer of '61.

And he wasn't alone.

Side by side was the man who batted behind him in the Yankees lineup, Mickey Mantle.

It is ironic that the villain in Maris's story was "the media," which made him a whipping boy for not being Mantle. Maris was swinging in the shadow of a designated hero. Mantle was only three years older than Maris but by then had been a Yankee for 10 years. He was the one who was supposed to finally fulfill his promise as heir to the great Babe and Joe DiMaggio. Maris, who had been touted as "a future Mickey Mantle" when he came to the majors with Cleveland in 1957, became a Yankee three years later.

The season before, in 1960, Maris hit 39 homers to Mantle's league-leading 40 and was voted most valuable player as the so-called M&M boys led the Yankees to the pennant. In those days, fans booed Mantle and cheered Maris.

As Maris and Mantle traveled across America knocking balls over the fence, Frick announced in July that any record broken beyond the 154 games of Ruth's schedule would bear an asterisk.

Maris's asterisk would remain until commissioner Fay Vincent had it removed in 1991, six years after Maris's death in 1985 at age 51.

Maris wore the mandated asterisk like a scarlet letter. His storied season was the first year of expansion to 10 teams in the American League and a 162-game schedule. Whereas Ruth had 678 plate appearances in 1927, Maris had 684 in 1961.

He was earning $42,500.

On September 10, his 27th birthday, Roger Maris had 56 homers; Mickey Mantle had 53. Then Mantle came down with a virus and soon was knocked out of the race.

After 154 games, Maris had 59 home runs. He tied Ruth with a homer off Baltimore's Jack Fisher on September 26. (It was Fisher's second time on the wrong end of history, having also served up Ted Williams's final home run.)

On the season's final day, October 1, in the fourth inning of a game against Boston in Yankee Stadium, where only 23,154 fans assembled to witness history, Maris became the single-season home-run leader with a blast off right-hander Tracy Stallard. It was the only run of the game.

Jack Fisher and Tracy Stallard would become teammates on the 1964 New York Mets.

To add to the irony, Roger Maris actually hit 62 home runs in 1961. One was washed out before a July 17 game in Baltimore became official. It would have been his 36th homer of the year. Of the 61 he hit that counted, 31 of them were on the road.

Roger Maris played just 12 seasons, and in only four of those could he muster even 500 at bats. He finished with 275 career home runs.

His career may have lacked longevity, but his record did not.

Sandy Koufax: The Left Arm of God (1963, 1965)

In his final six seasons in the major leagues, Sandy Koufax was superior, excellent, perhaps the best ever. Through the years thereafter, he became mythic and legendary.

Sanford Koufax was born a son of Brooklyn with big hands and long fingers and the God-given ability to throw the ball through a wall. Problem was the pitch would most times be high and outside. He was so wild that at Lafayette High School, he played first base while Fred Wilpon, the future owner of the Mets, would pitch. One day, Sandy Koufax would catch up.

He was also a gifted basketball player, good enough to win a scholarship to the University of Cincinnati. In college, he would pitch only four games before signing with his hometown Brooklyn Dodgers.

The ball club gave him such a large bonus that the rules at the time stated he had to be placed on the major-league roster. So, at age 19, instead of perfecting his craft in the minors, he sat on the bench in Brooklyn. In his limited opportunity, his wildness continued through six mediocre seasons.

That was until Dodgers catcher Norm Sherry got a hold of him in 1961. Sherry caught Koufax in a spring-training game against Minnesota and told him he didn't have to throw as hard as he could to be effective. Accordingly, Koufax slowed down and became more reliant on a curveball that dropped off a table. Thus began the career of the greatest left-handed pitcher of all time, who was about to cut a wide swath through baseball's record book.

At Yankee Stadium in the opening game of the 1963 World Series, Sandy Koufax established a new record with 15 strikeouts. Phil Linz was in the Yankees lineup that day and told me the ball had "jet propulsion," picking up speed as it got closer to the plate, not slowing down.

It was as if he were pitching in a higher league.

From 1961 through his final season in 1966, he was close to perfection. His 129–47 mark was complemented by a record five consecutive National League ERA titles, an MVP title, three Cy Young Awards, four strikeout titles, an 0.95 ERA in four World Series, four no-hitters in four years, and a perfect game against the Chicago Cubs in September 1965, during a season in which he struck out a then record 382 batters.

It is impossible to discuss Sandy Koufax without considering religion. His decision not to pitch the opening game of the 1965 World Series against Minnesota because it fell on Yom Kippur, the holiest day of the Jewish calendar, was reflexive for him but stunning to others. His decision was transcendent, transforming him from ballplayer to symbol, a standard to which all bar mitzvah boys and bat mitzvah girls are held. Funny thing is, he wasn't bar mitzvahed and did not attend services on the day he refused to pitch in Minnesota. But he did become an inadvertent icon.

Early in the seventh game, pitching on just two days of rest in the Twins' park, Koufax called out his catcher, Johnny Roseboro, to the mound. He told him all he had was a fastball and that would be the only pitch he would be throwing. In the span of two hours and five minutes, Koufax had 10 strikeouts and no walks in a 2–0 victory, and the Dodgers had their second world championship in three years.

That winter, when ownership still held sway in labor negotiations and players had no rights, Sandy Koufax did the unprecedented: he held out, in tandem with fellow future Hall of Fame pitcher Don Drysdale, in the joint hope of their becoming baseball's first $100,000 pitchers. Koufax ended the holdout when the Dodgers agreed to pay him $125,000.

That season, his final one, was statistically his best. Pitching through intense pain, shot up on codeine, enduring primitive treatments, he won 27 games, threw 27 complete games, and racked up 323 innings in the process.

Then, just like that, it was over.

No immortal in the history of baseball retired so young as Sandy Koufax. He was out at age 30 with an arthritic elbow hurting so much that he couldn't comb his hair without intense pain. He always said he never regretted the decision. He regretted having to make it.

Of course he was inducted into the Baseball Hall of Fame in his first year of eligibility, 1972, on the wings of the five best consecutive seasons a pitcher has ever had in the history of the game.

His pitching arm was so revered that it was often referred to as "the left arm of God."

Fred Wilpon once said he thought Sandy would never want to be remembered only by what he accomplished on the field. He may not want to admit it, but he also stood for values that he thought were important.

Those values are his legacy.

Purely Subjective List of the Greatest Relief Pitchers Since Ed's Been on Earth

Career save totals are given (qualification: minimum 300 saves—mostly), and active players appear in **boldface**.

Trevor Hoffman—591

Mariano Rivera—526

Lee Smith—478

John Franco—424

Dennis Eckersley—390

Billy Wagner—385

Jeff Reardon—367

Troy Percival—358

Randy Myers—347

Rollie Fingers—341

John Wettleland—330

Roberto Hernandez—326

Jose Mesa—321

Todd Jones—319

Rick Aguilera—318

Robb Nen—314

Tom Henke—311

Goose Gossage—310

Jeff Montgomery—304

Doug Jones—303

Bruce Sutter—300

Sparky Lyle—238

Hoyt Wilhelm—227

Elroy Face—193

CHAPTER 7
Managerial Strategies

◆◆

Two prerequisites for successfully serving as a manager are cooperating with the front office and earning the respect of the players. If a manager doesn't meet both of those requirements, then, boom, he is gone.

No questions asked.

If he can hold the job, he has three general areas of responsibility. Game strategy—the most visible of the three—makes a certain amount of difference, but I don't think any manager is going to turn his team around by his clever handling of a hit-and-run call.

Far more important than that is talent selection and utilization, the making of major decisions about who plays where and when.

Finally, the most important difference that a manager makes, I believe, is in setting the proper "emotional heat" for his ball club.

A baseball schedule does not permit the kind of emotional rhythm that organizes the life of a football player. You've got to go out and play to win seven days a week. It's a grind. In the course of that grind, it is just so easy to let things start to slide—to relax into an unself-conscious lethargy in which it ceases to matter whether the ball is cut off before it reaches the wall, and it seems to make no difference whether the runner who is ahead of you advances a base if you make an out.

When Jim Leyland or Bobby Cox or Tony LaRussa is around, you don't ever forget that it matters.

Years ago in Oakland, Billy Martin managed as if his hair and his team were on fire. The Athletics pushed convention and put constant pressure on the opposition. It was called "Billy Ball," and for a couple of seasons, it worked. Sad to say, what happened to Martin with the A's, as did habitually throughout his managerial career, was that Billy Ball became Billy Burnout.

The opposite of Billy Burnout would be the experience of Kansas City under Jim Frey. He inherited a team that, under the previous manager, Whitey Herzog, had overheated, a team that had too many emotions strained too hard. For one season, Frey was an excellent manager for that team. He guided his players through a cooling-off period in which they retained enough heat to cruise through the schedule. The problem was that Frey wasn't a low burner—he was an off switch. When he was fired, as when any manager is fired, it was widely reported that he was an innocent bystander, a victim of circumstances beyond his control.

Any manager who is a victim of circumstances should then be fired for being a victim of circumstances. *His job is to control the circumstances.*

Making a Difference

How much difference can a good manager make? I can't prove it, but I am absolutely convinced that a manager can have far more impact on his team's play than any player can.

Look at what Billy Martin used to be able to do. In stop after stop in his managerial career, player after player suddenly and dramatically improved his performance after Martin's arrival. When Rickey Henderson was inducted into the Hall of Fame, he said Martin "always got the most out of me." Henderson went on to credit Martin for teaching him "to compete at the highest level and respect the game of baseball," calling him "one of the best teachers and managers anyone could ever play for."

You think that's a coincidence? There is no record in baseball history of a single player's turning a bad team into a good team.

The best player might move a team from fourth place to second. Managers such as Martin have been known to move them from fourth to first. A manager is usually fired for cosmetic reasons—that is, to cover up the inadequacy of the front office. A large number of guys who become managers are capable of winning a pennant, providing that the players they have are better than those on the other teams.

Warren Spahn, a Hall of Fame pitcher, was talking about managers when he said, "I played for Casey Stengel before and after he was a genius." Stengel is in the Hall of Fame also, because of his managerial success with the Yankees, winning 10 pennants in 12 years with them, from 1949 through 1960. He did not go into the Hall because he managed the Braves or the Mets. He managed the Braves for six seasons in Boston and always finished in the second division, the bottom half of the league. Spahn pitched for him in the next-to-last one, 1942. He also pitched for him with the Mets in 1965. The Mets finished last, 10th, in each of Stengel's four seasons with them.

What Do Managers Do?

Managing might be the only job at which 100 million people would be competent but fewer than 10 are truly excellent. And half of them get fired anyway.

After all, what is it *exactly* that a manager does? The general manager makes the trades. The owner buys the free agents. The scouts spot the young talent. The pitching coach can change pitchers. The game's strategy hasn't changed in 100 years. The players play.

When Pat Corrales took over in Cleveland, he said, "I pat players on the back when they deserve it, and I get on them when they deserve it." In the history of baseball, this is part of its general wisdom. The trick is to employ it well.

Most baseball people know there are two other essential functions of a manager. The first is to keep the players, who can grow unhappy and frustrated at times over a period of eight months, from killing one another. The other is to keep the players from killing the manager.

As for strategy against the opposition, the great Ted Williams, who managed the struggling Washington Senators—and moved with them when they became the Texas Rangers—for four seasons, said, "There were times when I kept thinking maybe I should have done a particular thing differently. But, hey, there are two ways to play everything. And they're usually 50-50."

One time Don Zimmer, who had been fired several times in his managerial career, was asked why he got to the ballpark so early. "I want to make sure," he said, "that nobody is in my uniform."

A manager is a symbol of competence and authority on one hand. Yet on the other, he is indisputably a person who has put himself utterly at the mercy of events that he barely influences.

Who does that to himself?

That's baseball. And that's why managers, as a group, have so little dignity. Their professional fate is in the hands of people who are, in some sense, their inferiors. Gene Mauch, who managed the Phillies, Expos, Twins, and Angels, once said, "The worst thing is the day you realize you want to win more than the players do."

Stengel again: "Ability is the art of getting credit for all the home runs somebody else hits."

Managing in the major leagues is a stressful job—always has been.

The Dodgers' Hall of Fame manager Walter Alston, known as the "Quiet Man," took part in a 1968 experiment to measure the effects of occupational stress on the heart. As his club played the Giants, electrodes were placed on his chest and connected to a battery underneath his uniform. He was outwardly calm, but at critical points during the game, his heartbeat increased by 30 percent—to more than a hundred beats per minute.

Managing is such a rotten way to make a living, it's a shame so many nice people go into it.

Decisions, Decisions

From the nice guys to the task masters, all managers make decisions that affect the action on the field. Here's a rundown of some of them:

Why Would You Intentionally Walk a Batter?

You intentionally walk a batter when, in the judgment of the manager, your team stands a better chance of retiring the following batter.

An intentional pass may also be issued to set up a double-play possibility by putting a runner on first base.

If you had $100 for every time the following hitter felt disrespected and foiled the strategy with a hit or home run as retribution, you could retire.

Beyond the Box Score

Barry Bonds holds the records for intentional walks in a game, season, and career. He is one of six players in major-league history to be walked with the bases loaded to force in a run. It also happened to Josh Hamilton, of Texas, in 2008.

When Does a Suicide Squeeze Make Sense?

If a team is trailing by a run or two late in the game and has a runner on third base, a suicide squeeze might make sense.

What happens is, as described in Chapter 1, the runner on third breaks for home with the pitch, and the batter squares to bunt. If the batter fails to make contact or pops the bunt up, the runner is dead (hence the suicide). If, however, the batter bunts the ball fairly, the runner can score before any fielder can get to the ball.

It also works well if your team is leading by one or two runs and, if executed well, is easier than waiting for the batter to hit a fly ball or get a base hit to drive in the run.

The optimum time to do so is with one out.

What Happens When There's a Double Switch?

The double switch occurs when the manager removes his pitcher as well as one of his position players. It is a phenomenon principally of the National League.

As a hypothetical example, Ed Randall is a National League pitcher—*don't I wish*—who is due up at bat in his typical ninth position in the order. It's late in the contest, there's one out, and Ed has pitched another laudable game, but the score is tied at 1–1. The manager pinch-hits for Ed, whose lifetime average is way south of the Mendoza Line (a batting average below .200—an unfortunate reference to the light-hitting infielder Mario Mendoza, who actually finished his career at .215), bringing in a reserve outfielder who gets a single. The next batter, the leadoff hitter, also singles, with the pinch hitter stopping at second. The second-place hitter flies to left, and the runners hold. The third-place hitter, the center fielder, flies to center for the third out, ending the inning. In the double switch, the pitcher coming in to relieve Ed can be put in the third spot in the order, replacing the center fielder, while the outfielder who batted for Ed remains in the game as the center fielder, batting ninth. The new order, in effect, hides the pitcher, who is usually the weakest hitter in the lineup.

Hit-and-Run

With a runner on first base, and usually with fewer than two out, managers will call for the hit-and-run to stay out of a double play, since it reduces the time a fielder has to get the runner at second base.

It's risky, because putting the runner—or runners, as the case may be—in motion leaves the batter in a compromising position with regard to selectivity. He is now forced to expand his strike zone in an attempt to put the bat on the ball.

If the defensive team senses an oncoming hit-and-run, it may call for a pitchout, and the advancing runner may then be thrown out at second base.

Risk aside, if the hit-and-run works and the batter is successful in getting a hit, it will, more often than not, produce runners at the corners—first and third. Not only that, but also, in the act of covering the bag to receive a potential throw from the catcher, one of the middle infielders will be pulled out of position, creating a larger "hole" for the batter to hit the ball through.

For all the excitement of seeing this play in motion, rarely does it generate a team's run production. Most often, it puts two offensive players in a compromising position. The hitter is forced to expand his strike zone in an attempt to make contact with the ball, and the runner is often thrown out at second if the hitter cannot make contact, either because he did not take a traditional approach to stealing the base or because he's not fast enough to steal.

Critics say hit-and-runs exist only to convince fans that managers play a significant role in the outcome of a game.

Defensive Replacements

A team will replace a player in the field with one from the bench if the manager deems that the original player is a defensive liability.

It takes place only when the team is ahead or tied late in the game. The positions where defensive replacements are used most are first base and the outfield.

Beyond the Box Score

A few years ago, the Mets employed a first baseman named Mo Vaughn. He was highly paid for his bat, not for his glove. Vaughn was late in his career, and whatever defensive ability he once possessed had disappeared. Routinely, if the Mets were winning late in the game, the team would replace Vaughn at first base with a younger, more nimble defensive player at a high-traffic position, in an attempt to protect the lead.

Bringing the Infield In

A manager will instruct his infielders to play closer to home plate—on the lip of the infield grass—to try to choke off a run at the plate. The first and third basemen will play even with their respective bases rather than the customary few feet behind the bag.

As an option, the infield will be brought in by the defensive team's manager on those occasions when his team is trailing by no more than three runs in the fifth inning or later and there is a runner at third base, or runners at second and third, with no more than one out.

The infield may also be brought in when there are runners at first and third base with fewer than two outs and the defense is trailing by one or two runs in the eighth inning or beyond.

The strategy behind playing the infield in has less to do with retiring the batter than with increasing the probability that the runner at third base will have to remain there or get thrown out at home plate when the ball is put in play on the ground, because of the closer proximity of the infielders to the catcher.

All of this will go for naught if the ball is hit hard on the ground right past one of the infielders, who will have less time to react now that they are positioned closer to the batter.

Although it is sometimes said that by bringing the infield in you transform .200 hitters into .300 hitters, that is an exaggeration. In reality, averages will rise, but hitters don't stand a significantly better overall chance of getting a hit with the infield in.

In other words, by bringing the infield in, the defensive team risks sacrificing both a run and the out on a play that the player would have made if he were positioned normally.

A manager must decide when desperate times call for desperate measures.

Tagging Up

Tagging up allows a base runner to advance to the next base once a fly ball has been caught.

The rule is that a runner must return to the base he was occupying at the time the fly ball was hit. The runner must have at least one foot on the base at the instant the ball is caught and then is eligible to advance to the next base should he choose to do so.

Note that if the fly ball is caught in foul territory, the rule remains the same.

If the ball is hit far in the air and is caught a good distance from home plate, runners often advance one base without there being a play made on them. Conversely, if it is a short fly ball, runners will stay at their bases.

If a runner appears to leave his base prematurely, before the ball is caught, and never goes back to touch the bag again, the defensive team can stage an appeal play. The umpire will call the runner out regardless of what the runner had done while the ball was in play. Any runs that scored on the play before the appeal will count.

The best advice for base runners is to be sure to read the play well and watch the ball. You need to see the play yourself and not be reliant on your coach to communicate what to do.

And never, ever make the first or third out at third base!

Swinging on a 3-and-0 Count

Never, except if your team or the opposition is winning by many runs.

Sacrifice Bunt

If there's a runner on first base with fewer than two outs, the sacrifice bunt may be in order.

The threat of the bunt will keep the defenders in motion and, in doing so, make the double play more difficult to execute or open up a hole that ordinarily may not be there.

Bunts can come in handy late in close games where a club is playing for one run to tie or break a tie, or to add on to a one-run lead.

There is a risk for the fielder if, after fielding a bunt, in his estimation he has time to get the lead runner at second base. If he doesn't execute and throws the ball away, both runners will have reached safely.

Shifts

The strategy of shifting a third infielder to join the other two on their side of the infield to counter the threat presented by a hitter whose power is consistent to one side (a lefty who regularly hits the ball hard to right field, for example) dates back at least to the days of Ted Williams in Boston, against whom it was applied by Cleveland manager Lou Boudreau in July 1946.

In the 1960s, San Francisco's power-hitting first baseman, Willie McCovey—who, as with Williams, was an inveterate pull hitter (a lefty who regularly hit the ball with power to right field) and who, matching Ted, hit 521 home runs—was victimized similarly by the "McCovey shift."

David Ortiz, Ryan Howard, Jason Giambi, and Mark Teixeira are just four current players who, in the opinion of the opposition team, dictate a defensive alignment of three infielders on the same side of the infield.

For some reason, the shift is the province of left-handed batters. All of the four players cited are such, with Teixeira a switch-hitter who does not receive the same treatment when he bats right-handed.

On the shift, the third infielder is the third baseman, leaving the shortstop to guard a lot of territory on the remaining side of the field.

Righty/Lefty

Casey Stengel angered some of his players because he chose to platoon them—using different starters for the same position depending on the circumstances. His decision was based on the premise that it's easier for a left-handed hitter to get a better swing against a right-handed pitcher, and for a right-handed hitter to swing more effectively against a lefty. The logic behind this is that the lefty batter has a better line of sight to follow a ball leaving the hand of a right-handed pitcher, and vice versa. It may only be an extra fraction of a second, but considering how little time a batter has to react, it's enough to make a statistical difference more often than not.

Casey Stengel, a bust as manager with the Brooklyn Dodgers and Boston Braves, won 10 pennants in 12 seasons with the New York Yankees from 1949 to 1960. His philosophy was thus: on your 25-man team, there are 15 of them who don't care one way or another about you; the key to success is to keep the five guys who hate you away from the five guys who love you. Stengel's Yankees had a rare wealth of talent at most every position, and platooning was a way for worthy players to get into the lineup. On the downside, it angered many team members who would have played regularly with other clubs, other less successful clubs.

Building a Lineup

Here's some of the logic behind the decision made for each of the lineup spots. Of course, logic doesn't always apply, as Billy Martin famously pulled the lineup for his Yankees out of a hat for a game in the 1977 season in an attempt to end lackluster play.

Leading Off. It's customary for the first, or leadoff, hitter to be among the fastest runners and to have a discerning enough eye to swing only at strikes. His ability to run is secondary, though, to his ability to get on base by whatever means possible as often as possible. One of the only things significant about a batting order is the leadoff man must be good at getting on base and excel at making contact. Of the first five hitters, the first batter should be the one with the least amount of power and the most walks. Again, he must be good at getting on base.

Number Two Hitter. Up second is the so-called table setter for the middle-of-the-order batters, numbers three through five, coming next. This batter must protect the runner on base and be able to "handle the bat," allowing the runner to steal bases. He is a good hitter overall, has good bat control for sacrifice bunting, and isn't one of the top power hitters on the team.

Jim Gilliam, of the Los Angeles Dodgers, was one of the game's top number two hitters. In 1962, his protection helped leadoff hitter Maury Wills to steal a then record 104 bases.

Number Three Hitter. The team's best overall hitter goes third. The ideal is that this player hits consistently, for average, as well as for power. No small ball here.

Number Four Hitter. A typical number four hitter is big, slow, and, more than anyone else on the team, capable of hitting the long ball.

Number Five Hitter. Batting next should be one of the team's best hitters who can also hit for power. The fifth hitter could easily bat third, and vice versa: the player with more home runs could bat third, and the batter with more singles and doubles fifth.

Numbers Six, Seven, and Eight Hitters. The quality of the hitter should generally decrease through these spots in the order.

Number Nine Hitter. Generally, this is where the worst hitter on the team is slotted. On occasion, a manager might use this slot for a player with leadoff abilities, figuring that after the team goes through the order once, the number nine hitter is just as able to set the table for the big hitters in the middle of the lineup as the number one hitter.

Signs

Some signs are oral—for example, the third-base coach saying something to the batter. Hundreds of other signs are flashed every inning.

The manager signals the third-base coach that a play is on, let's say a double steal, by touching his cap; the third-base coach alerts the batter and the base runners by running has hand across the front letters of his uniform. At the same time, the catcher asks for a pitch with a sign, flashing down fingers to call the pitch and its location; the second baseman and the shortstop pick up the catcher's signs and relay them to the other fielders, giving everyone an idea as to where a batted ball might most likely end up.

All of this business is accompanied by espionage as complicated as that in a spy novel. When the bases are loaded, the third-base coach will emit more signals than a satellite sending to your GPS device. Hidden among those gestures, and the odd shout, are four basic messages: take, steal, hit-and-run, and bunt.

Over the years, coaches have devised all kinds of elaborate systems for relaying signs. They use decoys. They dance, jiggle, and jerk in the coaching box. They practice psychological warfare. Sometimes they defeat themselves with their own intricacy.

You can tell that a coach's signals are too complicated when a batter steps out of the box and his eyes are turning around like roulette wheels.

The key is to make the signs as simple as possible.

Steals

More than a generation ago, in 1980, American League players stole 1,455 bases and National Leaguers 1,839 among 26 total teams.

In 2000, with 30 major-league clubs, American League players stole 1,297 bases and their NL counterparts 1,627. That's 29 fewer stolen bases per club.

So, has the steal lost its appeal among managers and players?

In the early to middle 1990s, teams made a concerted effort to shut down the running game. That trend continues, but occasionally, we see a reflection of the past.

For example, early in the 2009 season, Dexter Fowler, of the Colorado Rockies, stole 5 bases in a game. Carl Crawford, of Tampa Bay, outdid that feat by swiping 6; he was successful on his first 28 stolen-base attempts and was at one point on pace to reach 100 steals (he finished the season at 60).

Adding to the thievery, Houston's Michael Bourn and Boston's Jacoby Ellsbury each stole home the old-fashioned way (as opposed to running on a wild pitch or a passed ball); they simply looked at the pitcher still holding the ball and ran, daring him to beat them to the plate.

Exceptions aside, the days of stealing a base—never mind a run—continue to vanish as the lust for the long ball grows. The home run is king. It's turned baseball into a station-to-station game of waiting for the homer.

Smaller stadiums conducive to home runs, along with bigger batters, quicker bats, first-base coaches with stopwatches measuring a pitcher's delivery, slide steps (which cut down that delivery time), and an overall change in managerial strategy have reduced a once integral part of scoring to an afterthought. In the process, the pure base stealer has become a relic celebrated only in record books, not on the field.

The players who used to be your slap-and-run hitters—your second basemen and shortstops—are home-run hitters now. Rarely, if ever, do you see teams playing for one run early in the game by using productive outs to advance a lone runner.

Baseball can change in subtle ways.

Almost all pitchers now use slide steps more often and are being taught in the minor leagues to use quick moves to the plate to guard against runners' gaining big leads. Just as important, if not more so, managers aren't willing to run when a power hitter is a batter or two away. Instead of stealing, would-be base stealers wait patiently.

Moreover, every runner on first is nowadays held on by the first baseman.

Teams are hesitant to try to advance 90 feet on a play at the risk of an out. Why chance it if the next batter might hit a home run?

As noted, in the 1990s, an explosion of offense began, causing teams to cut back on steal attempts. Teams really began making an effort to take away the running game, and the trend has continued ever since. That's why we don't see as many steals anymore.

During the 1960s, when runs were difficult to come by, the stolen base became a weapon. By the early 1970s, it had become an integral part of the game.

Stolen bases are up negligibly from the 2000 season, which is considered the peak of the steroid era. During the period 2003 to 2005, base stealing reached its lowest level since 1973.

You will no longer find consensus from baseball philosophers that establishing a running game is a priority in assembling a productive offense.

Chicks, along with most everyone else in the game, dig the long ball.

Stealing Second Base. Stealing is most effective when a team is ahead, tied, or behind by no more than a run or two.

To increase the chances of success, it is best if the batter is swinging at the pitched ball to protect the runner. The movement of the swing can momentarily distract the catcher from making an effective throw to get the runner.

With the first baseman holding him on, the runner needs to take as big a lead off the bag as possible to shorten the distance to second. The ideal is to stay just close enough to first so that when the pitcher throws over, the runner can retreat with only one step or a short dive. When doing so, you reach for the corner of the bag nearest the outfield (and farthest from the pitcher).

When taking a lead with the intention of stealing second, the base runner needs to "read" the pitcher to determine whether he will throw over or go home with his pitch. If the pitcher is right-handed, the runner should focus on the right heel or left knee; likewise, if the pitcher is left-handed, the runner should focus on the left heel or right knee.

To try to prevent the steal, the catcher will have a special signal to flash to his pitcher for a pitchout.

Here, the pitcher will intentionally deliver the pitch high and wide away from the batter. The catcher will step out of the catcher's box and, with no interference from the batter, throw unencumbered to second base.

Ordinarily, if there is a right-handed batter in the box, the second baseman will take the throw. If the batter is left-handed, it is the shortstop's responsibility on the receiving end. Late in a close game, starting the runner from first base in an attempt to steal second is a gamble: a manager must weigh the possible benefit of moving a runner into scoring position, from where he could reach home on most hits, against the disadvantage of running into an out on the caught-stealing play.

Stealing Third Base. A runner at second base needs to take the largest lead possible if the intention is to try to steal third base.

It is the responsibility of the third-base coach to watch where the shortstop is, as the runner has his back to him. The runner, meanwhile, must be vigilant of the positioning of the second baseman so that the fielder does not sneak back to the second-base bag for a pickoff attempt from the pitcher.

It is immaterial here whether the pitcher is left-handed or right-handed. Once the pitcher has come to the set position, the runner needs to concentrate on the pitcher's back leg, because he has to lift his foot from the pitching rubber in order to turn and throw.

When you're running to third, the objective is to reach for the corner of the bag closest to the outfield.

Stealing Home. As discussed earlier, a steal of home is rare to see in the game today, even with the two committed thefts during the 2009 season. When it happens, as a straight steal of home, it is usually the result of the third baseman's positioning. A runner on third will stray as far from the base as the third baseman, so the deeper the fielder plays, the bigger the runner's lead.

A runner with a big lead will sometimes dance around, making false breaks for the plate to either induce the pitcher to balk or desensitize him for what's coming. From there, it's all guts and gusto, followed by a cloud of dust.

Speed Demons—Some Guys Who Could *Really* Run

Career stolen-base totals are given.

Rickey Henderson—1,406

Ty Cobb—892

Tim Raines—808

Vince Coleman—752

Willie Wilson—668

Maury Wills—586

The New Century's Stolen-Base Leaders

National League

2001: Juan Pierre, Colorado; Jimmy Rollins, Philadelphia—46

2002: Luis Castillo, Florida—48

2003: Juan Pierre, Florida—65

2004: Scott Podsednik, Milwaukee—70

2005: Jose Reyes, New York—60

2006: Jose Reyes, New York—64

2007: Jose Reyes, New York—78

2008: Willy Taveras, Colorado—68

2009: Michael Bourn, Houston—61

American League

2001: Ichiro Suzuki, Seattle—56

2002: Alfonso Soriano, New York—41

2003: Carl Crawford, Tampa Bay—55

2004: Carl Crawford, Tampa Bay—59

2005: Chone Figgins, Anaheim—62

2006: Carl Crawford, Tampa Bay—58

2007: Carl Crawford, Tampa Bay; Brian Roberts, Baltimore—50

2008: Jacoby Ellsbury, Boston—50

2009: Jacoby Ellsbury, Boston—70

CHAPTER 8

Momentous Moments—
Divisional Play
(1968–1975)

◆◆◆◆◆◆◆◆◆◆◆◆◆◆◆◆◆◆◆◆◆◆◆◆◆◆◆◆◆◆◆◆◆

Professional football was gaining prominence in the 1960s with a second professional league and record TV ratings, and the NBA was on the rise, but baseball was in trouble.

The phenomenon of pitchers dominating the hitters peaked in 1968. Detroit's Denny McLain won 31 games, becoming the first pitcher to win 30 games since 1934. Bob Gibson, of the St. Louis Cardinals, compiled an earned run average of just over one run per game, 1.12. Somehow, he lost nine games that season. McClain and Gibson were the poster boys for the Year of the Pitcher, along with Cleveland's Luis Tiant with his 1.60 ERA.

Carl Yastrzemski, of the Boston Red Sox, batted .301 that season. That may not seem like a big deal, but he was the only player in the American League to bat above .300. Danny Cater, of the New York Yankees, was second at .290. To restore offense, the pitching mound was dropped by a third, from 15 inches to 10 inches. Since 1968, it's been all about the hitters.

Baseball has legislated nonstop against pitchers ever since, ushering in smaller ballparks, baseballs more tightly wound, and a strike zone that future Hall of Fame pitcher Greg Maddux has called "the size of a postage stamp."

In the fall of 1968, the NL and AL expanded by two teams apiece. The American League went back into Kansas City, abandoned since the Athletics moved to Oakland after the 1967 season. The Seattle Pilots were also born.

Gross mismanagement was the reason the Pilots lasted only one season. They were sold and moved during spring training in 1970, bought out of bankruptcy by a car dealer named Bud Selig, the proud new owner of the Milwaukee Brewers.

The National League expanded to San Diego and into Canada for the first time, placing a team in Montreal.

Formerly 10-team leagues, the American and National split into East and West divisions with six clubs apiece, introducing a League Championship Series as a qualification for advancing to the World Series.

In the first year of the new format, the New York Mets, having finished in last place every year since their birth in 1962 except for one when they finished next to last, defied odds of 10 bazillion to 1 and won the World Series. Amazin'!

Expansion was on the dance card yet again after the 1976 season for the American League. The AL followed the NL into Canada with the birth of the Toronto Blue Jays and gave Seattle a second chance with the Mariners.

The American League played through the 1980s with 14 clubs, the National with 12. After the 1992 season, the National League became the equivalent of the American League by expanding into Miami with the Florida Marlins and to Denver with the Colorado Rockies. For one year, each league continued to play with two divisions and the play-off format enacted in 1969.

But It's Only an Exhibition Game! (1970)

The reigning president of the National League used to go into his league's clubhouse at the All-Star Game and implore the players to take the game seriously and play hard. Even if it didn't count in the standings.

Nobody had to tell Pete Rose, who was nicknamed "Charlie Hustle" for a reason.

The American League led the 1970 All-Star Game on the evening of July 14 at newly christened Riverfront Stadium in Cincinnati by a score of 4–1 heading to the last of the ninth inning.

The National League rallied with three runs to tie the game and force extra innings.

In the 12th inning, hometown hero Rose singled and then moved to second on a base hit by the Dodgers' Billy Grabarkewitz. Facing Clyde Wright, of the California Angels, Chicago Cub Jim Hickman singled to center. Rose, rounding third base and determined to score and end the game, barreled into catcher Ray Fosse, of the Cleveland Indians, as the ball arrived from Amos Otis, of the Kansas City Royals, sending Fosse sprawling and dislodging the ball.

The National League had its 5–4 victory, its eighth straight, and Fosse, a rising young star, had a visit to a local hospital for observation.

Power to the People:
Flip On the Lights, Won't Ya? (1971)

Lights came to the major leagues in 1935 in Cincinnati. It was almost two generations later when light came to the postseason.

Charlie Finley, the cantankerous, garrulous owner of the Oakland Athletics, had been agitating his fellow owners and the baseball commissioner to play the jewel games of October after dark. His reasoning was simple: play the most important games of the year before the largest potential television audience.

Baseball eventually adopted Charlie's idea, and on October 13, 1971, a Pittsburgh-record 51,378 fans jammed Three Rivers Stadium for Game 4 of the World Series against Baltimore, which held a two-games-to-one lead.

For a night in mid-October, the weather in western Pennsylvania was remarkably cooperative, with the mercury at 72 degrees and the winds calm.

The novelty of the game was overshadowed by the choice of starting pitcher by Pittsburgh manager Danny Murtaugh. He selected Luke Walker, who had not pitched in three weeks. Earlier in the season, Walker had enraged the Pirates manager by failing to disclose a sore arm, but he came back to win five consecutive decisions in August and September.

The decision to start Walker looked as if it would implode when the first three batters he faced all singled, loading the bases. All three went on to score, for a 3–0 O's lead, and Walker was gone.

But that would be all the runs they would get as rookie Bruce Kison burst onto the national stage pitching shutout ball.

Pittsburgh's Buccaneers rallied for two runs in the bottom of the first, followed by single runs in the third and seventh innings, and went on to defeat Baltimore 4–3, outhitting the O's 14 to 4, to square the Series at two games apiece. Pittsburgh would eventually win the Series in seven games.

Almost 40 years later, World Series games are now played exclusively at night after having been played during the daytime since 1903. The last World Series day game was played indoors, when the Cardinals met the Twins at the Metrodome for Game 6 of the 1987 series. Three years earlier, the Tigers and the Padres played during the day in games four and five of the 1984 World Series—the last series to feature a game played beneath an open afternoon sky.

The Abomination Called the Designated Hitter (1973)

Baseball was ruined in 1973 by the installation of an abomination entitled the designated hitter. It had become, embarrassingly, the only sport with a split personality, featuring two sets of playing rules.

Actually, the DH had its origins generations before, as far back as 1906. In an attempt to increase offensive production, Philadelphia Athletics manager Connie Mack suggested using a 10th player, who would bat in place of the pitcher.

At the annual MLB meeting on December 1, 1928, National League president John Heydler offered a substantial rule change. He proposed the use of a "designated hitter." He argued that it would speed up the game and eliminate the problem of weak-hitting pitchers.

The National League voted to approve the idea, but the American League said no. The idea, ahead of its time, was not enacted.

In the early 1970s, baseball faced a crisis of popularity. Offense was at its lowest ebb in generations. In 1968, the entire American League batted just .230. Some 20 percent of games in the major leagues that year were shutouts.

Then, on January 11, 1973, at a joint meeting of owners, all 24 representatives approved the use of a designated hitter in the American League, starting that season in a three-year experiment. It was the first time since 1901 that the American League and National League played under different rules.

The impact was immediate. After AL teams had averaged 3.47 runs per game in 1972, the number jumped to 4.28 in the first year of the DH. The league batting average jumped from .239 to .259.

In addition to boosting the average number of runs scored per game, the DH prolonged careers. Hank Aaron, having broken Babe Ruth's career home-run record, returned to Milwaukee for a final season as a DH. Later, the DH extended the shelf life of aging sluggers such as Reggie Jackson, Carl Yastrzemski, Frank Robinson, Orlando Cepeda, Tony Oliva, Rico Carty, Tommy Davis, Harold Baines, and Hal McRae, among countless others.

In 1976, the DH was used in the World Series for the first time. It was in place in even-numbered seasons.

The rules changed again for the 1986 Fall Classic: the home team for each game determined which rules would be applied.

That practice remains in place today.

In 2004, the Hall of Fame welcomed Paul Molitor, its first inductee to compile more lifetime at bats as a DH than in any other position.

Seattle's Edgar Martinez spent almost his entire career as a designated hitter. Will he join Molitor one day in Cooperstown?

I don't mean to suggest there's a consensus on the matter of the DH. Rather, the once warring factions in the game—the AL loves it, the NL loathes it—have simply agreed to disagree.

The best chance for change came in the early 1990s when baseball went to three divisions per league and realignment between the leagues was on the table. Later, when two expansion franchises in Tampa Bay and Arizona were introduced in 1998, and radical realignment was again under consideration, eliminating the DH was a part of the discussion.

Had there been a full-scale overhaul of leagues and divisions, the DH almost certainly would have been legislated out of existence in the interest of harmony. As it turned out, the overhaul boiled down to Milwaukee's moving from the American League to the National, and the impetus for change disappeared.

Called Shots Too bad the broad overhaul—and consequent demise of the DH—never happened. If you're going to play 10 players on a side, then just call it softball and put a keg of beer out behind second base, OK? (Whattaya really think about it, Ed?)

The Wildest Trade in New York Yankees History (1973)

In 2006, a major New York paper listed the top one hundred fascinating, random facts about New York City baseball. Finishing first was this fact: two pitchers on the 1973 New York Yankees, Fritz Peterson and Mike Kekich, swapped wives, children, and dogs, too.

There was more: houses, cars, insurance—everything.

Really. A reality show long before there was such a concept for television shows.

This wasn't a wife swap; it was a life swap.

The pitchers started their unique version of switch-hitting in October 1972. It was left to Yankees manager Ralph Houk to call in the press during spring training in 1973 and inform reporters of a most unusual trade.

The media representatives were blindsided, flabbergasted as to how to handle such an unprecedented story.

On March 6, 1973, the *New York Times* ran the story on page 51.

Page 51!

If you're scoring at home, Peterson traded his wife, Marilyn, along with two kids and a poodle, to Kekich for his wife, Suzanne, their two kids, and a terrier.

The word that commissioner Bowie Kuhn used to describe his reaction was *appalled*. Get this: he reportedly received more angry mail about the Kekich-Peterson trade than he did about the introduction of the designated hitter one month later.

Peterson clearly got the better of the deal. At this writing, he and Suzanne are still together after 37 years. Kekich, meanwhile, split with Marilyn three months after the couples went public.

For the good of the team, the Yankees shipped Kekich to Cleveland in the middle of the '73 season.

Adding a dash of irony to the mix, Peterson also went to Cleveland. In April 1974, he was one of four pitchers the Yankees dealt in a widely unpopular trade in New York for Chris Chambliss and Dick Tidrow, building blocks central in the team's return to prominence just a couple of years later.

By that time, though, Kekich had moved on to Texas. He made only eight more starts in the majors. Peterson had two years left in him, going a combined 24–25 for Cleveland and later Texas during that period, including a 14–8 season for the Indians in 1975, when he threw nine complete games and finished the year with a 3.94 ERA.

Can you begin to imagine how big this story would be if it broke today in our YouTube and Twitter world?

Homage to Hank (1974)

For a kid who started out batting cross-handed for the Indianapolis Clowns in the Negro Leagues, Hank Aaron did quite well, don'tchathink?

Coming out of the cauldron of great baseball talent that was Mobile, Alabama, Henry Louis Aaron was quiet, unassuming, and shy.

Notwithstanding, no one in the second half of the 20th century exerted more influence on the record books. He mesmerized teammates with a soft-spoken dignity that defined his off-field personality for almost a quarter century while delivering a less subtle message with the booming bat that earned him baseball immortality.

That the home-run record would become Henry Aaron's legacy seemed preposterous when the skinny, six-foot-tall, 17-year-old boy who once played second base left his poor neighborhood in Mobile with two dollars, a tuna fish sandwich, and a cardboard suitcase.

No one could have envisioned the unflinching work ethic and competitive fire that would allow Hammerin' Hank to produce a one-time-record 755 home runs over a career that started in 1954 with the Milwaukee Braves, for whom he hit 723 homers, and ended 23 seasons later with the Milwaukee Brewers, for whom he swatted 32 more, mostly as a designated hitter.

Hank Aaron was a right-handed hitter with a fluid swing and lightning reflexes, but his secret was in the wrists. Powerful wrists allowed him to keeps his hands back and drive the ball to all fields with tremendous force off his front foot.

Taken individually, the numbers were never spectacular: eight 40-homer seasons, never more than 47 homers in a year; 11 100-RBI seasons, never more than 132 at a clip. The spectacle is in the bottom lines: third all-time in hits; tied for third with Ruth in runs scored; first in runs batted in, total bases, and extra-base hits; a .305 career average with a couple of batting titles thrown in; and, of course, 41 more home runs than the legendary Babe Ruth. The man who hit 20 or more homers in 20 consecutive seasons also appeared in 24 All-Star Games, a record he shares with Willie Mays and Stan Musial.

In 1957, his lone MVP season, it was Hank Aaron's home run in the 11th inning that clinched Milwaukee's first pennant.

Among all these accomplishments, never did he receive more attention than when it became apparent he would exceed the lifetime home-run total of the mythic Ruth.

In the summer of 1973, he received as many as three thousand letters a day. Many were filled with hateful and racist language and even included threats on his life. An Atlanta policeman, Calvin Wardlaw, was assigned to provide him with around-the-clock protection, keeping a snub-nosed .45 handgun in a binocular case.

Aaron refused to ride in convertibles, in restaurants always sat facing the door, and would say later, "This changed me."

Hank Aaron began the 1974 season one home run shy of Ruth's 714. The Braves opened on the road, and the world did not have to wait long for him to buggy-whip that powerful bat through the strike zone. In the first inning, facing Jack Billingham at the Cincinnati Reds' home field, he connected on his first swing of the season to tie the mighty Bambino.

After he rounded the bases, he was mobbed by teammates and greeted by commissioner Bowie Kuhn, who had ordered him to play on the road (Aaron had hoped to complete the milestone before an Atlanta home crowd), as well as by vice president Gerald Ford.

On April 8, 1974, in the Braves' first home game of the season, Hank Aaron became the new all-time home-run champion with a blast off of Al Downing, of the Los Angeles Dodgers.

Aaron's daughter, a college student and the subject of a possible kidnap threat, had to watch the triumphant moment on television while under the protection of FBI agents. His mother hugged him after he touched home plate, still fearful that someone might try to shoot him.

When he stepped to the microphone during a brief on-field ceremony that stopped the game, these were his words: "Thank God it's over."

Lost in the shadow of the home-run mountain that Henry Aaron finally scaled was the athlete's all-around consistency. He had outstanding speed, good instincts, and one of the game's better arms from right field, tools that earned him three Gold Gloves.

Barry Bonds exceeded Hank Aaron's home-run record, but 755 will forever endure as one of the game's magical numbers, just like 714. It is a lasting monument to an underappreciated star and to the courage and integrity with which he played the game.

To many, he will always be the all-time home-run king.

Body Language (1975)

The Boston Red Sox captured the imagination of the baseball world in 1975 with their first appearance in the World Series since 1967 and only their second since 1946.

They trailed the Big Red Machine of Cincinnati three games to two and were losing Game 6 by a score of 6–3 when pinch hitter Bernie Carbo hit a three-run homer with two outs in the bottom of the eighth inning to tie it.

Carlton Fisk, of Charlestown, New Hampshire, a town of about a thousand people, told me his high school team had played as few as eight games in a season and his graduating class had 38 students. Charlestown High had only three boys' sports, one for each season. The baseball team played on a converted pasture with no fences. When there wasn't a game, cows grazed there. Early in the season, chunks of ice would have to be chopped off the trees near the field so as not to have the branches hanging over the foul lines.

He dreamed of playing power forward for the Boston Celtics. Instead, he hit a home run that most people can only dream about.

More than four hours after the game's first pitch, he left the on-deck circle to start the bottom of the 12th inning telling teammate Freddy Lynn, "I'm going to hit one off the wall. Drive me in."

Facing Cincinnati pitcher Pat Darcy, Fisk golfed a low, inside sinker into the New England night down the left-field line. The only question was: fair or foul?

He slowly made his way up the first-base line, waving his arms, urging the ball to stay fair, iconic gyrations frozen in time and forever attached to baseball's history.

The ball struck the foul pole and bounded back onto the field.

Home run!

It was indeed, winning the game and forcing a seventh game. The Fenway organist burst into the "Hallelujah" chorus of Handel's *Messiah*.

Fisk later commented, "If everybody who mentioned to me they had been at the game were truly there, there'd be eight hundred thousand people at that game. My only regret is that it didn't happen in the seventh game. But as everybody in Boston knows, the Red Sox won that Series three games to four."

To honor one of the most thrilling home runs in Boston history, the left-field foul pole in Fenway Park—whose complement in right is known as the Pesky Pole after Johnny Pesky—was christened the Fisk Pole.

Purely Subjective List of the Greatest Fielders Since Ed's Been on Earth

Players are listed alphabetically by position, and active players as of this writing appear in **boldface**.

C—Johnny Bench, Charles Johnson, Yadier Molina, Tony Pena, Ivan Rodriguez, Manny Sanguillen, Benito Santiago

1B—Keith Hernandez, Don Mattingly, Wes Parker, Vic Power, George Scott, J. T. Snow

2B—Roberto Alomar, Nellie Fox, Bobby Grich, Bill Mazeroski, Manny Trillo, Frank White

SS—Luis Aparicio, Mark Belanger, Larry Bowa, Ozzie Smith, Omar Vizquel

3B—Clete Boyer, Graig Nettles, Ken Reitz, Brooks Robinson, Aurelio Rodriguez, **Scott Rolen**

LF—Joe Rudi, Carl Yastrzemski

CF—Jim Edmonds, **Ken Griffey Jr.**, **Torii Hunter**, Andruw Jones, Gary Maddox, Willie Mays, Dwayne Murphy, Gary Pettis, Vada Pinson

RF—Roberto Clemente, Andre Dawson, **Vladimir Guerrero**, Roger Maris, Al Kaline, Dave Parker, Dave Winfield

CHAPTER 9

Stats—Keeping Score, Sabermetrics, and Fantasy Baseball

Is it true that, as we often hear, baseball is dull?

No, baseball is only dull to dull minds. The good news is that an instant elixir is at hand for those who think nothing is going on when plenty is: paperwork. Learning how to score can unlock the hidden pleasures of baseball and enhance your enjoyment of the game.

The scorecard is a baseball fan's fingerprint. The completed cards may all look alike at first glance, but try to find two that are exactly the same. Fans develop their own nuances for recording the game's play-by-play. Only one rule is unbreakable: use a system you can decipher later. It can be as simple as "1B" for single and "FO" for fly-out. Once you get started scoring, though, you're probably going to want to do more.

Trust me: you'll be addicted.

What All the Stats and Abbreviations Mean

Here's the basic shorthand for what happens during the game and the stats we use to measure the results:

BB   Base on balls

BK   Balk

CS   Caught stealing

DP   Double play

E   Error

F   Fly-out (or just the position number of the player who caught the ball)

FC   Fielder's choice/force-out

FO   Foul fly-out

HP   Hit by pitch

K   Strikeout

L   Line-out

PB   Passed ball

SAC Sacrifice bunt

SB   Stolen base

SF   Sacrifice fly

WP   Wild pitch

For Hitters

Official At Bats (AB). The basis for all batting statistics. All at bats are official at bats except for walks, sacrifice bunts and flies, catcher's interference, and hit by pitches.

Take your turn at the plate. Play in all 162 games in a major-league season and you'll accumulate about 680 of these.

Plate Appearances (PA). More than at bats, PAs include walks, sacrifices, hit by pitches, and—my favorite—catcher's interference.

Batting Average (BA). This value traditionally has determined the worth of a hitter. It is calculated by dividing the number of hits by the number of official at bats. Thus, if a batter has 30 hits in 100 at bats, he's hitting .300. (EDitorial: if you're playing for the Holy Family Club in the senior division of the University Heights Little League in the Bronx, and you get three hits in 28 at bats—two of them bunts—that's a sparkling .108 average. But note it was a *hard* .108.)

On-Base Percentage (OBP). A much better indication of a batter's worth than simply his batting average. It is calculated by dividing the number of times a batter reaches base in all the ways a batter can reach base—hits, walks, hit by pitches (but not including reaching by error, fielder's choice, reaching first on a dropped third strike, or being awarded first base by interference or obstruction)—by his number of at bats, walks, hit by pitches, and sacrifice flies (but not including sacrifice bunts). This stat is particularly important in determining the effectiveness of leadoff hitters. An on-base percentage of approximately .360 is the dividing line between good and bad.

Runs (R). The number of times you score.

Runs are a very underrated statistic that have only recently begun to receive the respect they deserve. And remember: you can't score if you first don't get on base. Right, Yogi?

Runs Batted In (RBI). The batter is credited with an RBI if a run scores as a result of a hit, a walk with the bases loaded, a sacrifice or sacrifice fly, an infield out (double play exempted), a fielder's choice, or—again, my favorites—catcher's interference or obstruction.

Total Bases (TB). The total number of bases created by base hits. Thus, if a batter accumulates one of each of the possibilities during a game—a single, a double, a triple, and a home run—he would have 10 total bases (1 + 2 + 3 + 4). This particular example is called "hitting for the cycle."

Slugging Percentage (SLG). The average number of bases a batter achieves per official at bat. It's determined by dividing the number of total at bats into his total bases. Thus, if a batter has 25 at bats and he accumulates one of each of the possibilities—single, double, triple, and home run (10 total bases)—in that period, he has a slugging percentage of .400.

For Pitchers

Earned Run Average (ERA). A reliable indicator of a pitcher's efficiency. It is calculated by multiplying the total number of earned runs allowed by 9 (the standard number of innings per game) and then dividing that figure by the total number of innings pitched, including fractions of an inning.

If I pitched nine innings and gave up three earned runs, my ERA would be 3.00. All runs are earned runs unless an error was committed, allowing the runner to score, and/or there was a passed ball, catcher's interference, or obstruction. Thus, if I pitched the same nine innings, but one of the runs scored when an error was committed with two outs, that would be considered an unearned run, which would lower (i.e., improve) my ERA to 2.00.

Holds (H). An unofficial statistic credited to a relief pitcher who enters a game with a save opportunity and maintains the lead until he is replaced by another pitcher.

Innings Pitched (IP). Each out recorded is a third of an inning. If a starting pitcher departs in the eighth inning with one man out, he is credited with having pitched seven and a third innings.

Quality Starts (QS). A starting pitcher earns a QS if he has pitched at least six innings and allowed no more than three runs.

Saves (S). *The* stat for closers. Let's refer to the 2009 edition of the Official Baseball Rules, rule 10.19 in particular: The official scorer shall credit a pitcher with a save when such pitcher meets all four of the following conditions:

1. He is the finishing pitcher in a game won by his team;

2. He is not the winning pitcher;

3. He is credited with at least ⅓ of an inning pitched; and

4. He satisfies one of the following conditions:

   a. He enters the game with a lead of no more than three runs and pitches for at least one inning;

   b. He enters the game, regardless of the count, with the potential tying run either on base, or at bat or on deck (that is, the potential tying run either is already on base or is one of the first two batters he faces); or

   c. He pitches for at least three innings.

Wins (W) and Losses (L). The record of a pitcher, with wins appearing before losses. A pitcher can be credited with a win if he is the starting pitcher who pitches at least five innings and leaves with his team having a lead that is never relinquished, or if he is a relief pitcher who enters the game with his team tied or behind and is the pitcher when his team scores the eventual winning run.

The losing pitcher is the one responsible for the base runner who scores the eventual winning run. (If anybody cares: in my best season ever, I was 12–1—with a 1.53 earned run average.)

Called Shots

The introductions of both the five-man rotation and pitch counts (tracking—and limiting—how many pitches are thrown in an outing) have conspired against a pitcher's winning 20 games in a season. The same goes for losing 20 games in a season; the last to do so was Brian Kingman for Oakland in 1980.

Keeping Score

A standard scorecard format is shown in Figure 9.1.

To begin, you fill out the far-left column with the lineup order for that day, followed by each player's number in the next column. Then label each defensive position with its corresponding number, 1 through 9 (as shown in the following list). As you watch the game, each box on the scorecard represents what that batter did in his plate appearance that inning. If the batter didn't come up to bat, the box stays blank. Here are the position numbers:

1—Pitcher   6—Shortstop

2—Catcher   7—Left field

3—First base   8—Center field

4—Second base   9—Right field

5—Third base

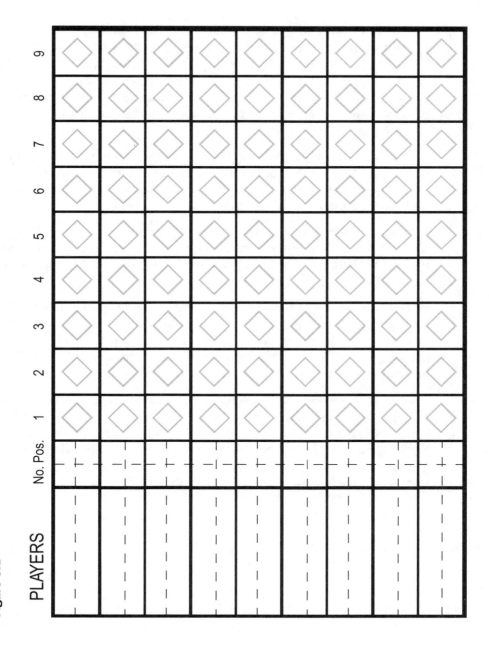

Figure 9.1

The position numbers are also used to record outs by the respective opposition players. For example, when a player hits a fly ball to left field that is caught, put "7" (or "F-7") in the box by his name in the corresponding inning. If he grounds to the third baseman, who throws him out a first, the out is recorded "5-3." Figure 9.2 gives you an idea of how it all works; here, a generic team has batted through the first two innings.

It gets a little more involved when a batter reaches base. Each corner of the box represents one of the bases. Many fans use the lower left-hand corner as home, lower right as first base, upper right as second base, and upper left as third base.

When a batter singles, enter one tiny line in the corner designated for first base. On a double, enter two lines in the corner for second base. On a triple, enter three lines for third base, and for a home run, use four lines.

You can leave it at that, or you can chart the progress of the runner around the bases. Some scorers do that by tracing a line from base to base (some scorecards have a diamond outline within the square to make it easier). Others do it by penciling in the uniform or position number of the batter who moved the runner along.

So, if Derek Jeter singles, you'd put one line in the first-base corner. If he goes to third on a single by left fielder Johnny Damon, you'd add a "7" (or Damon's uniform number, "18") in Jeter's third-base corner. Let's say Jeter is thrown out trying to steal second while Damon is up. You'd put "CS 2-6" or just "2-6" (catcher throwing to the shortstop) in the second-base corner, where the action took place.

Figure 9.2

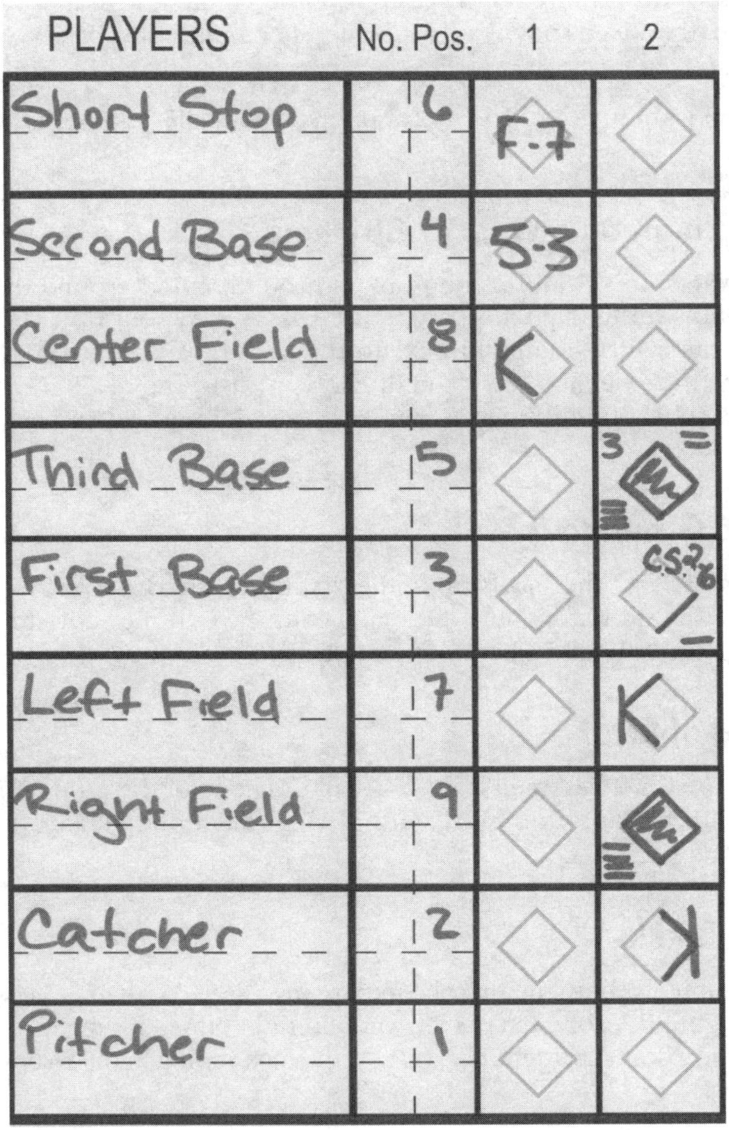

PLAYERS	No. Pos.	1	2
Short Stop	6	F-7	◇
Second Base	4	5-3	◇
Center Field	8	K	◇
Third Base	5	◇	◈
First Base	3	◇	CS.2 6
Left Field	7	◇	K
Right Field	9	◇	◈
Catcher	2	◇	K
Pitcher	1	◇	◇

When a runner scores, some scorekeepers circle the scoring play, while others fill in the diamond created by the runner's trip around the bases so they can spot it at a glance. Those are the basics of scorekeeping.

Now, if you want to get a little more sophisticated, let's go inside the numbers.

Note the Count on a Walk or Strikeout

If a batter walks on a 3-and-2 count, put a little diamond around the BB. If he walks on four pitches, circle the BB. A strikeout on a 3–2 count warrants a little diamond next to the "K" (not around it). A strikeout on three pitches gets a small check next to the "K," and a batter who strikes out looking (as opposed to swinging) gets a backwards "K."

Define the Groundout

OK, it went 6-3, from the shortstop to the first baseman. But if a ball is hit sharply to the shortstop, put a little line over the 6. If the shortstop has to charge the ball, add a half loop under the 6.

What Kind of Error

An error on the third baseman is "E-5"—but did he boot the grounder or make a bad throw to first? If it's a throwing error, put a small "t" next to the "E" ("Et-5").

Fill In the Blanks

You'll see squiggly lines in the accompanying New York Yankees scorecard, Figure 9.3, for each player who didn't bat in an inning. This ensures that you don't accidentally start off the next inning in the wrong box. A variation on this would be to block out the box of every player who didn't bat in that inning with a set of double crossed lines.

Other Scoring Habits
(Details, Details, and More Details)

Was it a ground single or a line drive? Did it go to the left or right? Lots of variations to recording this level of information are in use.

Here's one: If it's a ground single to center, put a "C" (or "8") below the line for the single. If it's a line (or fly) single, the "C" goes above the mark. An infield single to second base is shown by a "4" under the line.

Pencil or Ink?

Some folks color-code their system to get quick totals at a glance, a benefit that is especially important to me when I do play-by-play from the radio booth.

I use red for strikeouts, green for walks. Want my rationale? Don't laugh, OK? Green means go, red means stop.

Babe Ruth taught me that in 1918.

Kidding.

Others swear by the pencil. I'm cocky. I always use ink. But I do carry a bottle of correction fluid just in case.

Yankees Versus Orioles

Figure 9.3 is the New York Yankees score sheet from the May 10, 2009, game against Baltimore.

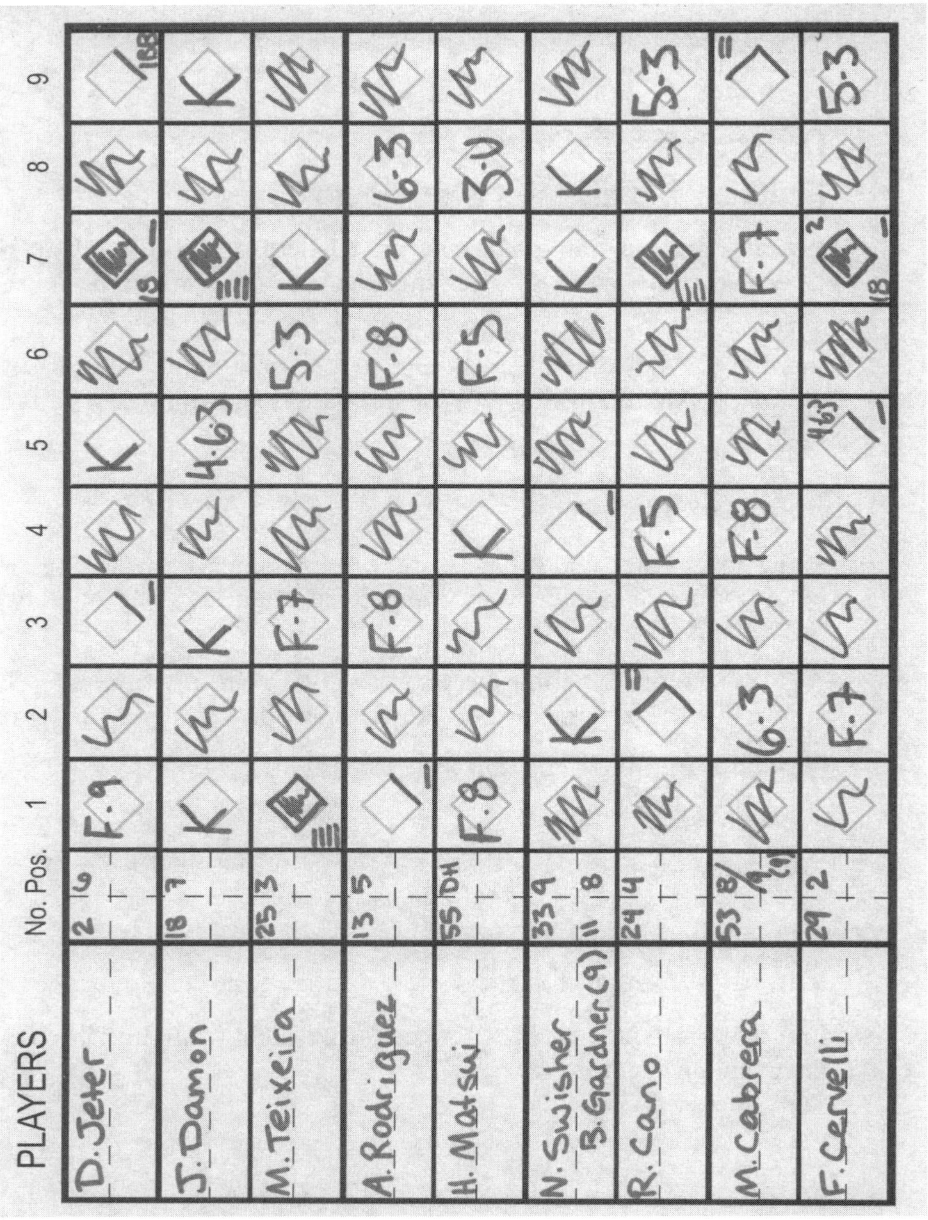
PLAYERS
No. Pos.
1
2
3
4
5
6
7
8
9
D. Jeter
J. Damon
M. Teixeira
A. Rodriguez
H. Matsui
N. Swisher
B. Gardner (9)
R. Cano
M. Cabrera
F. Cervelli

Figure 9.3

Here is a partial recap:

First Inning

Derek Jeter flies out to right fielder Nick Markakis. One out.

Johnny Damon strikes out swinging. Two out.

Mark Teixeira homers to right center field.

Alex Rodriguez lines a single to left field.

Hideki Matsui flies out to center fielder Adam Jones. Three out.

Totals: One run, two hits, no errors, one man left on base

Second Inning

Nick Swisher strikes out swinging. One out.

Robinson Cano lines a double to right field.

Melky Cabrera grounds out to shortstop, Robert Andino to Aubrey Huff. Two out.

Francisco Cervelli flies out to left fielder Felix Pie. Three out.

Totals: No runs, one hit, no errors, one man left

Third Inning

Derek Jeter lines a single to left field.

Johnny Damon strikes out swinging. One out.

Mark Teixeira flies out to left fielder Felix Pie. Two out.

Alex Rodriguez flies out to center fielder Adam Jones. Three out.

Totals: No runs, one hit, no errors, one man left

Fourth Inning

Hideki Matsui strikes out swinging. One out.

Nick Swisher grounds a single to right field.

Robinson Cano pops out to third baseman Melvin Mora. Two out.

Melky Cabrera flies out to center fielder Adam Jones. Three out.

Totals: No runs, one hit, no errors, one man left

OK, runner at first with one out. The batter hits a ground ball to second base. The second baseman turns and throws to the shortstop at the second-base bag, who touches second to get the approaching runner from first. The shortstop throws the ball to the first baseman before the batter arrives, for an inning-ending double play. Score it "4-6-3" on your card, otherwise known as the pitcher's "best friend."

Sabermetrics

Sabermetrics is the science of answering questions about baseball through the analysis of the statistical evidence. Its name comes from the Society for American Baseball Research, SABR for short.

Bill James, one of the most well known sabermeticians and currently working in the Red Sox front office as a senior advisor, is generally credited with lifting the science of statistical research to this completely new level. James's *Baseball Abstract*, published from 1977 to 1988, consistently exposed the fallacy behind the box score. James believed that too much importance is placed on a player's batting average—a manipulated number that undervalues walks and extra-base hits—and not enough on his ability to get on base. Thus, the statistics we're accustomed to appreciating aren't the ones that actually matter.

Thanks to his revolutionary work, major-league teams routinely employ specialists whose sole responsibility is to provide reliable analysis of their players and the opposition. Without exaggeration, James is almost certainly one of the most important baseball minds of the past quarter century.

The Seattle Mariners, long considered to be in the dark ages when it came to the new generation of modern-day statistics, now have a full-time three-man staff that develops and analyzes statistics as part of the routine player-evaluation process.

Pat Gillick, general manager of the 2008 world champion Philadelphia Phillies, used statistics as one tool, one part of the evaluation of players, while maintaining a strong belief in the core value of having a scouting staff adept at seeing strengths and weaknesses in players, regardless of their stats. He never formally embraced the use of sabermetrics to the degree that the Red Sox did—Boston went so far as to place Bill James on staff—but Ruben Amaro Jr., who replaced Gillick upon his retirement, entertained the thought of hiring someone for statistical analysis of the Phillies players and their opponents.

James's ideas found a wide audience among baseball fans who play fantasy baseball, but the people who ran real professional baseball teams, at first, dismissed James and his followers as numbers-obsessed freaks. It took a high school–educated former number-one draft choice of the New York Mets who ascended to the general manager's chair of the Oakland Athletics to develop a parallel universe where the old rules no longer applied.

Billy Beane, operating in a small market with limited financial resources, reaped extraordinary success with a new kind of baseball knowledge, a rethinking of the way the game is perceived and played. As the major leagues' leading practitioner of James's statistical philosophy, Beane was roundly hailed as the game's newest genius, bucking the odds and becoming baseball's most surprising success story with the second-lowest payroll in the game.

Beane knew all about the conventional way of assessing players. Using himself as an example, a much sought-after player with unlimited potential who ultimately flamed out after six seasons and in just shy of 150 major-league games, he recognized that talent wasn't enough to overcome a chronic lack of discipline at the plate. Beane, assisted by Ivy League–educated assistants, assembled a team packed with intelligent players who knew how to work a count, how to wear out a pitcher and wait for him to make a mistake.

Billy Beane's approach to evaluating talent within the game was the subject of Michael Lewis's 2003 book *Moneyball*. The book also helped popularize a stat that combined on-base percentage with slugging percentage, referred to as OPS (OBP plus slugging).

The result? The triumph of originality and the centerpiece of a baseball revolution. This accomplishment sparked an explosion of interest in statistical analysis of baseball. It's credited largely to the rise of rotisserie and fantasy baseball, but it is also due to increasing fan interest in baseball knowledge for its own sake.

Fantasy Baseball

There is some dispute about the date and site of the birth of fantasy baseball, in which fans manage imaginary teams that they compile based on the real-life performances of major leaguers.

Conventional wisdom holds that it debuted in 1980 when a group of baseball fans, including writer Daniel Okrent, founded Rotisserie League Baseball during a lunch at a Manhattan restaurant called La Rotisserie Française.

Disputing that notion is William Gamson, an adjunct professor at Boston College. He claims fantasy baseball was already 20 years old when the boys went to lunch in New York City. Gamson and a few friends started the National Baseball Seminar based on individual statistics.

The two games are not duplicates of each other.

For one thing, the NBS relies on just four statistics—runs batted in, batting average, earned-run average, and games won. Rotisserie uses multiple stats.

Rotisserie and fantasy baseball exploded in the age of the Internet. Prior to the formation of online leagues, "owners" would phone in their lineup changes or send them through the mail; the input was all compiled and then scored by a league commissioner, who would provide regular updates. Today, courtesy of the Internet, league sites allow daily transactions and changes up until game time.

How Do You Draft a Fantasy Baseball Team?

In the interest of full and complete disclosure as I attempt to dispense my best advice regarding winning at fantasy baseball, I hereby admit to having never played it in my life (as a journalist, I have too many friends and acquaintances on too many teams).

That said, as The World's Foremost Authority, it is my advice that you take three items to your draft: a set of roster sheets to fill in; a list of eligible players that you have previously ranked, divided by position; and a current injury list.

If you load up with a lot of other stuff, there's too much to keep track of and get distracted by.

Keep it simple.

If you're having trouble deciding between which of two players to select, flip a coin.

Kidding.

Equipping yourself with as much pertinent information as you can in a condensed format will limit the second-guessing.

If you need a second baseman but you also need a third baseman, see how many of each have been taken by your competitors. Opt for the position player selected the least amount of times. Also, keep an eye out for players who qualify at multiple positions.

Depending on your league's rules, a player such as San Francisco's Pablo Sandoval may qualify as a catcher even if he's been behind the plate for only a handful of games. Sandoval has also put in time at first base and third base, meaning that not only can you get his power in your fantasy lineup every day as a catcher without having him suffer from the wear and tear common to the position, but also you can plug him into a corner infield slot should you have an injury.

Most standard leagues start off as "5 × 5" leagues, crediting owners for five offensive categories (RBIs, runs, average, home runs, and steals) and five pitching categories (ERA, wins, saves, strikeouts, and walks plus hits divided by innings pitched—WHIP). Fantasy scoring will give the poorest performer in each category 1 point, with an additional point for each position up the ladder (so, in a 10-team league, the league leader in home runs gets 10 points). Rotisserie scoring may weight some categories more than others. Either way, in order to accumulate those points, you need to have players in your lineup before a given game, keeping several on the bench for you to second-guess yourself later with what could have been.

Here are some other attributes to keep in mind as you prioritize your draft and set your lineup:

Efficiency. Players who cover multiple stats (e.g., guys with speed who can hit for power) are coveted properties, as they make the best use of limited lineup space.

Home Team. A decent pitcher on a team with a lousy bullpen may not get his fair share of wins. Similarly, a slugger in a weak lineup may not get as many RBI opportunities as his stats from previous years say he's capable of amassing.

Playing Time. Watch out for platoon players. If they're not in the major-league lineup, they're not earning you points.

Depth. When it's late in the draft and you've already missed out on that aging closer who spent some time on the disabled list (DL) late last season with "arm fatigue," be sure to keep an eye on his team's eighth-inning guy, as that guy could be first in line to take over the job should it become necessary.

Surgery. Remember that impressive hitter from two years ago who had surgery and kind of fell off the radar last year as he worked his way back to form? He could be due and, at the least, might make for a solid sleeper pick.

Opposing Pitcher. As you operate your team day to day, think like a big-league manager (that is where the fantasy in fantasy baseball comes in). If you've got a lefty outfielder going up against Randy Johnson in his prime, maybe that's the night to play one of your reserve guys instead (at one point lefties were hitting a lifetime .199 against the Big Unit).

Opposing Catcher. Similarly, if you've got a speedster on your team who is only in your lineup to get you more stolen bases, and his team is playing the Twins tonight, perhaps let Joe Mauer catch him stealing on your bench (given that as of the end of the 2009 season, Mauer has nailed 38 percent of the would-be base stealers he's come up against).

Ballparks. Windy day at Wrigley? Any day at New Yankee Stadium? Maybe consider going with another starting pitcher rather than a guy prone to fly-ball outs.

Who Are Today's Best Players?

Thanks to a thoroughly unscientific survey, here are the best of the best in 2009 by position:

SP—Roy Halladay, Toronto Blue Jays

C—Joe Mauer, Minnesota Twins

1B—Albert Pujols, St. Louis Cardinals

2B—Chase Utley, Philadelphia Phillies

3B—Alex Rodriguez, New York Yankees

SS—Hanley Ramirez, Florida Marlins

LF—Ryan Braun, Milwaukee Brewers

CF—Torii Hunter, Los Angeles Angels

RF—Ichiro Suzuki, Seattle Mariners

RP—Mariano Rivera, New York Yankees

CHAPTER 10

Momentous Moments— the Dawn and Rise of Free Agency (1976–1993)

Three days before Christmas in 1975, an arbitrator rendered a decision that forever changed baseball and the business of sports: he created free agency.

A man named Peter Seitz, then baseball's impartial arbitrator, created free agency when he supported a grievance filed by two players, Andy Messersmith and Dave McNally.

Messersmith was a pitcher for the Los Angeles Dodgers who played the 1975 season under a contract that had been renewed. He did not sign a new contract because the Dodgers refused to give him a no-trade clause. McNally, who pitched for the Montreal Expos, also played that season with a renewed contract, until he retired that June.

Seitz found that the renewal clause in players' contracts lasted for only one year, not in perpetuity, and when it expired, so did the players' links to their teams. The so-called reserve system, the 65-page opinion said, did not enable a team to retain a player with whom it did not have a contract.

No pronouncement has had more impact in professional sports. The decision may also make for the most important labor-arbitration case, because it has resulted in a greater transfer of wealth from ownership to employees than in any other case.

Either side, the players or the owners, could unilaterally fire the arbitrator, with no reason needed.

The owners did just that to Seitz right after he handed down the decision.

Mark Teixeira ($180 million over 8 years), C. C. Sabathia ($161 million over 7 years), and Alex Rodriguez ($275 million over 10 years), Yankees all, owe a sizable debt of gratitude to Peter Seitz, a man they possibly never have heard of.

Chris Chambliss Gets (Lots of) Help Rounding the Bases (1976)

Chris Chambliss never touched home plate.

He missed second base, too.

On October 14, 1976, the son of a minister and first baseman for the Yankees hit one of the most dramatic home runs in the history of October baseball and in the august history of Yankee Stadium.

The League Championship Series games were best-of-five before expanding to best-of-seven in 1985. With New York and Kansas City tied at two wins apiece and at 6–6 in the bottom of the ninth inning, Chambliss led off against Royals reliever Mark Littell and launched a high fastball into the right-field bleachers to send the Yankees to their first World Series in 12 years.

It also sent thousands of fans onto the field in raucous celebration.

Fans were racing everywhere by the time Chambliss turned first base. He tripped near second base trying to navigate through a sea of humanity.

The bases and home plate had been lifted off their moorings.

And not by the grounds crew.

A former football player, Chambliss forearm-shivered a few fans en route to the Yankees dugout.

Once inside the safety of the clubhouse, he was asked by his teammates if he ever touched home plate.

So, Chambliss called for some protection.

He took off his uniform jersey, put on his jacket, found the two biggest cops in Yankee Stadium, put one on either side of him, and rejoined the mayhem. They made their way to home plate, or where home plate once stood. Chambliss put his foot on the indentation of the plate, turned around, and went back inside.

It counted.

Reggie! Reggie! Reggie! (1977)

One of the game's emblematic sluggers, Reggie Jackson was traded by the Oakland A's to Baltimore in May 1976.

In the new age of free agency, the A's knew they would never be able to meet Jackson's contract demands.

Nor could Baltimore.

That fall, the Yankees returned to the World Series for the first time since 1964 only to be humiliated by the Cincinnati Reds, losing four straight games.

The tempestuous owner of the Yankees, George Steinbrenner, was determined to do whatever it took to fortify his club.

Reggie was at the top of that list.

The romancing of Jackson was handled by the owner himself, who signed him to a five-year, $2.8 million deal, big dollars then.

Jackson would later say that Montreal and San Diego actually made better financial offers in pursuing him.

The Yankees returned to the World Series in 1977 and got ahead of the Dodgers three games to two with an opportunity to close it out at home.

In batting practice, Reggie hit practically every pitch into the seats and appeared to be locked in for the kill.

Dodgers starter Burt Hooten walked Jackson on four pitches in his first at bat. Perhaps Hooten had seen the show Jackson put on in BP.

When Jackson came back up in the fourth, Hooten tried to come up and in but didn't get it up enough. Reggie hit a home run to right field.

The next inning, with Elias Sosa on in relief, Jackson again homered, a blistering line drive again into the right-field seats and the hardest ball he hit all night.

As the crowd repeatedly chanted his name throughout the stadium, with the Yanks ahead 7–4 in the eighth inning and facing knuckleballer Charlie Hough, Reggie hit his most majestic homer, a drive deep into the unoccupied "black" in the center-field bleachers to punctuate the Yankees' World Series victory.

Three homers in one game by one man, the first such feat in a World Series since Babe Ruth, off of three different pitchers on just three swings.

He was made for the moment.

Ozzie Barehands—Who Needs a Glove? (1978)

It didn't take the San Diego Padres long to realize they had something special in their rookie shortstop, Ozzie Smith.

On April 20, 1978, as they were playing at home against Atlanta, the Braves' Jeff Burroughs hit a ground ball up the middle with two outs in the fourth inning. It appeared that it would go through for a base hit. Smith, who made more dives in his career than Michael Phelps, hit the dirt, glove extended.

But this time the ball took a bad hop and bounced up over him.

No problem. Smith reached back with his bare hand, caught the ball, and then climbed to his knees and threw to first base.

In plenty of time.

The fielding artistry of the Wizard was born, and he was on his way to 13 consecutive Gold Gloves at shortstop for defensive excellence.

Bucky Dent (1978)

On July 19, 1978, the Yankees were 14 games out of first place. Returning to the World Series to defend their championship seemed like nothing more than an improbable dream.

Improbable though it was, the Yankees proceeded to stage one of the most stunning pennant rallies in history. They caught and passed the Red Sox, only to have the Sox catch them on the final day, forcing a one-game play-off to determine the winner of the American League Eastern Division.

That's where Bucky Dent comes in.

When the Yankees acquired him from the Chicago White Sox, they thought they were getting a solid fielder and a fair hitter—he had hit only four homers all season and had never hit more than eight in a season.

The Yanks lost a coin toss and had to travel to Boston for the game.

October 2, 1978.

Thousands of Yankees fans know the date by heart.

So do thousands throughout Red Sox Nation.

Boston led late in the game behind Mike Torrez, the same Mike Torrez who caught the final out, a bunted pop fly, to culminate the 1977 world championship season for the Yankees before leaving for Boston through free agency.

The only reason Dent batted in the seventh inning of a game they were losing 2–0 was that they were out of spare infielders.

With two men on base, Dent represented the go-ahead run at the plate.

He fouled a ball off his foot. Hopping around in pain, he asked the trainer to come out and take a look. After walking around a bit, he decided he was OK and went back into the batter's box.

Mickey Rivers, the Yankees leadoff hitter, was on deck and had been closely observing Dent the entire time. While nearly everyone else in Fenway Park was watching Dent grimace in pain, Rivers noticed that the bat Dent was using was the same one Rivers had used earlier in the game—and Rivers knew the bat was cracked.

He grabbed a batboy and sent him to the plate with the bat he was holding. Dent switched weapons in the middle of an at bat.

Then it all happened.

Torrez fired a fastball. Dent stepped back with his new bat and took an easy swing. Even in cozy left field, it at first appeared to be a pop-up. Torrez thought it was an easy out, just as most everyone else did.

They were wrong. The ball caught a gust of wind and neatly cleared the Green Monster.

Al Clark, the second-base umpire that day, said Dent's ball cleared the Monster, all 23 feet 7 inches of it, by maybe 2 inches.

That made the game 3–2 Yankees and an indelible entry in Yankees folklore.

It is ironic that Dent is remembered mostly for swinging from the heels, one of which was still throbbing from the ball he had fouled off of it on the previous pitch.

The Yankees won the game 5–4, beat Kansas City for the American League pennant, and rallied from a two-games-to-none deficit to beat the Los Angeles Dodgers for the second straight year to successfully defend their world championship.

And Bucky Dent was named World Series Most Valuable Player.

I Got It, I Got It, I Got It, You Got It (1980)

The Philadelphia Phillies were two outs away from their first world championship in 61 years in Game 6 of the 1980 World Series.

They were leading Kansas City three games to two and 4–1 with one out in the top of the ninth inning when Royals second baseman Frank White lifted a pop foul near the Phillies dugout on the first-base side. Catcher Bob Boone called for the ball. It dropped into his mitt but then bounced out.

Fortunately for the Phillies, the first baseman, Pete Rose, also gave chase.

He was standing beside Boone, and the ball rebounded from the catcher's glove into his. Two outs.

Tug McGraw followed up by striking out Willie Wilson for a Series-record 12th time, and the celebration was on.

Still the One and Only (1983)

Not one grand slam was hit in the first half century of All-Star Game play dating to its birth in 1933. That changed when the Chicago White Sox served as host on July 6, 1983, against the backdrop of 11 consecutive victories by the rival National League.

In 1975 with the Boston Red Sox, outfielder Fred Lynn burst onto the scene unlike any other major leaguer in history. He became the first player to be named Rookie of the Year and MVP in the same season. Imagine the expectations thenceforth.

He spent the rest of his career trying to duplicate the extraordinary success of that first season and was eventually dealt to the then California Angels in a blockbuster trade.

Lynn was selected to his ninth consecutive all-star team in 1983 but apparently still had not earned the enduring respect of opposing National League manager Whitey Herzog, even though he had hit four home runs and driven in 10 runs in just 20 All-Star Game at bats. Only Ted Williams had more all-star RBIs, 12, and that was in 46 at bats.

Herzog ordered Robin Yount walked intentionally to load the bases for Lynn in the third inning against starting pitcher Atlee Hammaker, who, as was Lynn, was left-handed.

When asked if he felt disrespected, Lynn said, "Yeah, I took it personally."

Hammaker tried to sneak a fastball by Lynn, and Lynn snuck it into the stands for the first grand slam in All-Star Game history.

This was the second time Lynn capitalized after the batter in front of him was walked intentionally to get to him. Playing for USC in 1972, he hit a three-run homer that knocked the University of Texas out of the College World Series.

The All-Star Game grand slam was the key to a seven-run inning—all seven charged to Hammaker—en route to a 13–3 victory and the AL's first all-star victory since 1971.

The Pine Tar Game (1983)

On July 24, 1983, a lazy Sunday afternoon at Yankee Stadium in the Bronx, Kansas City's George Brett hit a two-run home run off of Goose Gossage with two outs in the ninth inning to put the Royals ahead 5–4.

Apparently.

That lead lasted as long as it took Yankees manager Billy Martin to rush to home plate, claiming that the bat Brett used had pine tar above the legal 18-inch limit from the handle.

The bat was called for by home-plate umpire Tim McClelland, who examined it and then gave it to Joe Brinkman, the crew chief. They measured it against the 17-inch-wide home plate and found that Brett's bat had pine tar at least 19 inches up, or 1 inch above the limit.

McClelland raised his right hand, Brett was called out, the game was over, the score reverted back to 4–3 Yankees, Gossage had his 12th save, and the game ended on a home run by the visiting team.

Enraged, George Brett rushed from the dugout to confront the umpires and had to be restrained by a number of Royals players.

Called Shots

To this day, I have never seen a player in uniform madder than George Brett was that day.

As Royals players spilled out toward home plate, Gaylord Perry wrestled the bat away from McClelland and handed it to teammate Steve Renko, who starting running toward the Kansas City dugout. He was chased into the runway between the dugout and clubhouse by stadium security men before surrendering it.

According to rule 1.10-b: "The bat handle, for not more than 18 inches from the end, may be covered with or treated with any material (including pine tar) to improve the grip. Any such material, including pine tar, which extends past the 18-inch limitation, in the umpire's judgment, shall cause the bat to be removed from the game."

The rules also imply that any ball hit by an illegal bat is an out.

Oh, by the way, the Yankees had known about Brett's bat since their last visit to Kansas City just a few weeks before.

Yankees third baseman Graig Nettles was familiar with the obscure rule because he'd seen his teammate Thurman Munson called out in Minnesota for the same thing about eight years earlier. He mentioned it to Martin, who stored the information until needed.

The Royals, of course, filed a protest with the American League immediately.

After an investigation was concluded, a press conference was called to announce the findings regarding whether the protest would be upheld.

I arrived with my ESPN camera crew to cover the press conference at the same time that American League president Lee MacPhail did. As we walked toward the building, I asked him what would happen. He said, "You might be surprised."

The president of the league overturned the umpiring crew's ruling and allowed Brett's home run to stand. Lee MacPhail explained that while pine tar was too high on the bat, "games should be won and lost on the playing field—not through technicalities of the rules."

He ordered the game resumed from that point on August 18.

With different umpires on hand, Martin started things off by protesting that Brett failed to touch all of the bases on his home run. In response, crew chief Dave Phillips produced a signed affidavit from the Brinkman crew affirming that both Brett and the base runner preceding him, U. L. Washington, had indeed touched all the bases.

To further signal his disdain, Martin played pitcher Ron Guidry in center field. He also gave us something else we had never seen before: a left-handed second baseman, none other than Don Mattingly (lefty fielders usually don't play second, as they have to turn their bodies around to throw the ball to first on a ground ball—including Mattingly, only six have done so since 1957).

George Brett was told to stay put on the Royals' charter at Newark Airport and was not involved in the four-out finale.

In hindsight, the entire incident could have been avoided if on-deck hitter Hal McRae had reacted more quickly. After Brett hit the homer, Billy Martin screamed to his batboy to retrieve Brett's bat. McRae said that, instead of thinking about a game plan against Gossage, he should have grabbed the bat and thrown it into the dugout.

The bat now resides in Cooperstown.

As a memento for covering the resumption of the game, members of the press received complimentary cans of pine tar.

I still have mine.

Unopened.

4,192 (1985)

Riverfront Stadium, Cincinnati, September 11, 1985.

San Diego's Eric Show throws a fastball, and Pete Rose slashes at the pitch, shooting a line-drive single into left field.

It was Rose's 4,192nd career hit, and before he reached first base, the capacity crowd was on its feet. For the next nine minutes, the stadium rocked from the thunderous applause directed at the man who had just broken Ty Cobb's all-time career hit record, a feat many fans had considered untouchable.

Those who saw Cobb play said he was possessed by a force demanding that he prevail. Not coincidentally, it was Rose who broke Cobb's record.

Whatever Rose lacked in natural ability—power, speed, agility—was overshadowed by his incredible drive. His career was a remarkable 25-year demonstration of excellence, willpower, and team loyalty that made his name synonymous with winning.

Batting and MVP titles were secondary to championships. He was the quintessential self-made man who played more for the love of the game than for money, an anachronism at a time of bigger and bigger paychecks and demands to match.

In the opinion of many observers, Rose not only was assured a place in the Hall of Fame but also would be remembered as one of the game's greatest and most respected players.

Less than four years later, Peter Rose was the subject of investigations from the commissioner's office as well as federal prosecutors. The multiple inquiries focused on an assortment of charges: illegal betting, including wagering on baseball; the sale of prized and bogus memorabilia; dealings in unreported cash and possible income-tax evasion; and associations with shady characters, such as convicted cocaine dealers and bookies.

For his indiscretions, Pete Rose was banned for life from baseball, including being made ineligible for the Hall of Fame, and eventually served time in jail in Illinois for tax evasion.

"Go Crazy, Folks, Go Crazy" (1985)

In his first season in St. Louis, Ozzie Smith's artistic play at shortstop helped the team bring home the 1982 World Series title—the Cardinals' first championship since 1967.

Three years later, he helped the Cardinals win another pennant, this time with his bat. In the fifth game of the best-of-seven National League Championship Series against the Los Angeles Dodgers, with the teams tied at two wins apiece and the score 2–2 in the bottom of the ninth inning, Ozzie golfed a pitch from reliever Tom Niedenfuer down the right-field line that soared over the fence just inside the foul pole.

Game over, and broadcaster Jack Buck told a national television audience to let loose.

What made it unique was that it was Smith's first career home run batting left-handed in what was then for him a total of 2,969 career at bats from the left side (in addition to his appearances through two postseasons) and just his 14th in his eight years in the majors to that point. He would hit only 28 regular-season home runs in his 19-year career (23 of them from the right side).

In 2005, the home run was voted the greatest moment in the history of Busch Stadium.

Ozzie was eventually named the NLCS Most Valuable Player after hitting .435 in the Cardinals' six-game triumph.

Why'd Ya Pitch to Jack Clark? (1985)

Ozzie's home run just described, one of the most unforgettable homers in St. Louis baseball history, led to another in the next game, the sixth of the NLCS, now in Los Angeles.

The Dodgers led 5–4 going to the ninth inning.

Two were out with the bases loaded and the tying run 90 feet away at third and the potential go-ahead run at second. The due batter was the only legitimate power source in the Cardinals lineup, Jack Clark.

First base was open.

But Tom Niedenfuer—yep, him again—had struck out Clark the last time up. Dodgers manager Tommy Lasorda decided to tempt fate and let Niedenfuer pitch to Clark.

Mistake, *really big* mistake!

Clark lit into a Niedenfuer fastball and hit it into the left-field pavilion at Dodger Stadium, 450 feet away.

The Cardinals now led 7–5.

The Dodgers went down in order in their half of the ninth, and the Cardinals moved on to the Fall Classic against cross-state rival Kansas City in the I-70 Series.

Well, He Sure *Looked* Out (1985)

The creed of umpires is to go about their business and never be noticed.

It's a worthy goal, but in Game 6 of the 1985 World Series, Don Denkinger couldn't help being noticed, making a call that would echo through Cardinals history for years to come.

The St. Louis Cardinals, playing in Kansas City, scored a run in the eighth inning and led 1–0 going to the bottom of the ninth.

Three more outs and the Cards would have their second world championship in four years.

Don Denkinger was in his 17th season as an American League umpire and 9th as a crew chief.

Notably, he was at first base and became embroiled in one of the most memorable moments in Series annals.

Cardinals closer Todd Worrell, facing the top third of the Royals order, got Jorge Orta to hit a slow rolling ground ball to first baseman Jack Clark. Worrell broke for the first-base bag to cover the play, and Clark tossed the ball to him.

Worrell tagged the middle of the bag.

Then Orta tagged it.

"Safe," Denkinger ruled emphatically, prompting a visit and vigorous argument from St. Louis manager Whitey Herzog, who was supported by TV replays.

With runners eventually at second and third, Dane Iorg singled to right to drive in both runs, and the Royals had a 2–1 win and life, sending the Series to a seventh and deciding game—which they also won, 11–0, for Kansas City's lone world championship.

Not only did baseball commissioner Peter Ueberroth chastise Denkinger after the sixth game, but also the ump was the victim of hate mail and death threats for two years. A pair of St. Louis disc jockeys had paved the way by giving out his address and phone number on the air. Denkinger would finish up his 30-season umpiring career 13 years later, retiring after the 1998 season.

Fernando Mania (1981–1986)

Mexico's greatest *beisbol* export, Fernando Valenzuela, electrified Southern California in 1981 as a 20-year-old left-handed pitcher with an aura of youthful invincibility on the mound.

He grew up in a town in Mexico so tiny that it could not be found on a map. Etchohuaquila, population 250, was adobe huts, dirt floors, no electricity, no running water. The youngest of 12 children, he left school after the sixth grade. He was 17 when a scout for the Dodgers found him, at which time he was making about $80 a month pitching.

After pitcher Jerry Reuss pulled a leg muscle 24 hours before his scheduled opening-day start, the Dodgers bravely gave the ball to Valenzuela, who only a day earlier had pitched batting practice. Nonetheless, he shut out the Houston Astros 2–0 on five hits.

By mid-May, he was 8–0 with an 0.50 ERA, and Fernando mania was sweeping the country.

Relying on a screwball that he had learned a year earlier, he threw seven complete games and five shutouts—including 36 consecutive scoreless innings—in those first eight starts.

He was the National League's starting pitcher in the All-Star Game and finished the season leading the league in strikeouts, complete games, and shutouts. He became the first player in either league to win Rookie of the Year and the Cy Young Award in the same year.

Valenzuela helped the Dodgers win the World Series and received a tidal wave of attention.

In the 1986 All-Star Game, played in Houston, Fernando Valenzuela tied the 1934 record of Carl Hubbell, of the New York Giants, by striking out five consecutive batters. It started with Don Mattingly and continued through Cal Ripken Jr., Jesse Barfield, and Lou Whitaker and concluded with fellow countryman Teddy Higuera.

Valenzuela ended the season leading the league with 21 wins and 20 complete games, the most since Sandy Koufax 20 years before.

Most important, his legacy was galvanizing the interest of millions of Latinos, a marketing juggernaut opening corporate America's eyes to the idea of marketing Hispanic players to an audience hungering for heroes.

It Ain't Over . . . (1986)

Among Yogi Berra's most famous sayings was this: "It ain't over till it's over."

Never was that observation more applicable than to the Boston Red Sox during the postseason in 1986. On a late Sunday afternoon, it appeared the California Angels were about to go to the first World Series in franchise history to play the New York Mets.

Just four years before, in 1982, the Angels were likewise one game away from the World Series, leading Milwaukee two games to one in the American League Championship Series, which was then a best-of-five match. Alas, the Brewers won the final two games and went to the Fall Classic instead.

Now the A's were leading the Sox three games to one in a best-of-seven play-off and were up 5–2 in the ninth inning of Game 5. Police had begun to descend into the Angels dugout to protect the playing personnel from the oncoming celebration. The players were starting to hug both each other and Gene Mauch, who had begun his managerial career in 1960 and was generally regarded as the best manager to never win a pennant.

Most of all, everyone was thrilled for the owner of the team, actor Gene Autry, considered the most benevolent and kindest in the major-league lodge.

It was then that a two-run home run by former Angel and MVP Don Baylor, virtually forgotten by what was to happen, cut the lead to 5–4.

When Dave Henderson stepped to the plate with two outs, there was a runner on first. In short order, he was down to his final strike.

The count was 2-and-2. Angels closer Donnie Moore threw a split-fingered fastball that was supposed to sink but didn't as much as it should.

Henderson lifts a fly ball to deep left field. Brian Downing retreats to the fence and watches in astonishment as the ball lands on the other side.

Anaheim Stadium is as quiet as high mass.

It's 6–5 Boston.

The home run by Dave Henderson flew into the pantheon of most dramatic home runs in the history of baseball, joining those hit by Bobby Thomson and Bill Mazeroski.

Two ironies:

First, Henderson was not in Boston's original starting lineup. He entered the game in center field as a replacement for Tony Armas, who had suffered a leg injury.

Second, he wanted to crawl into a hole after a play that occurred in the sixth inning. The Angels' Bobby Grich hit a drive to deep center. Henderson caught the ball on the run an instant before his momentum carried him into the wall. The ball was dislodged and dropped over the fence. That was a two-run homer, and it gave Anaheim a 3–2 lead.

Despite the shock of the two homers by Baylor and Henderson in the top of the ninth, the Angels tied it up in the bottom frame on a pinch-hit single by Rob Wilfong, scoring pinch runner Ruppert Jones. All the Angels needed was one run and the World Series awaited.

They loaded the bases with one out against Red Sox reliever Steve Crawford but could not convert, forcing extra innings.

In the 11th inning, it was Henderson against Moore yet again.

This time, the Sox center fielder hit a sacrifice fly to drive in the eventual winning run in a 7–6 victory, forcing the series to return to Boston.

Despite the crushing loss, the Angels needed only to win one of the possible two games to go to the you-know-what.

They didn't.

Dispirited, they were beaten twice in Boston, suffering the ignominy of being the team to get closest to the World Series—one strike away—without actually getting there.

Henderson, meanwhile, continued his magnificent play in the World Series. He batted .400, and his home run leading off the 10th inning in Game 6 at Shea Stadium gave Boston a lead that on any other night would have delivered the team's first world championship since 1918.

In a supreme irony, however, they were about to find out how the Angels felt.

"A Little Roller up Along First" (1986)

In his baseball life, Bill Buckner had few errors.

He was one of the most ferocious hitters in baseball since coming to the majors with the Los Angeles Dodgers. Buckner played in four decades. His 2,715 hits are more than Ted Williams or Joe DiMaggio could claim and more than the total of many others enshrined forever in Cooperstown. His .289 lifetime batting average was higher than Carl Yastrzemski's. He won a National League batting title with the Chicago Cubs in 1980 when he hit .324 and set a league record for assists by a first baseman. He was an all-star in 1981 and twice led the league in doubles, in 1981 and 1983. In a tape from April 1974, he can be seen climbing atop the left-field fence at Atlanta's Fulton County Stadium in a vain attempt to catch Hank Aaron's 715th home run. Two years later, he suffered a staph infection in his ankle, and after four operations, he basically played on one leg for the last 14 years of his career.

Buckner drove in 212 runs for the Red Sox over the previous two seasons, despite constant pain in his ankles. But all that good stuff was forgotten the instant that "little roller up along first" as described to a nationwide audience by the great Vin Scully on NBC, a sure out, somehow eluded Bucker and damned him with the scarlet letter of one of the undying mistakes in the realm of sports.

The Zapruder film of baseball.

As you recall from the preceding episode, Dave Henderson had just delivered at Shea. His leadoff homer was followed by a run-scoring single off the bat of Marty Barrett to put Boston two runs up, 5–3. Riding high now in the 10th inning of Game 6, Boston was poised to win the World Series.

Three more outs and the Curse of the Bambino, the explanation for the franchise's decades of futility following the trade of Babe Ruth, would be vanquished after 68 years.

Wally Backman flies out to left field. One out.

Keith Hernandez flies out to center field. Two out.

One out away!

Gary Carter singles. Kevin Mitchell singles. Ray Knight singles.

Ray Knight's single came on an 0–2 pitch. The Sox, harking back to the Angels, were a strike away.

Carter scores. It's 5–4.

Pitching change.

Wild pitch scores Mitchell. Tie game.

Bob Stanley engages Mookie Wilson in a 10-pitch duel.

With a full count of 3-and-2, Wilson taps—all together now—"a little roller up along first. *Behind the bag*, it gets through Buckner—here comes Knight and the Mets win it!"

Trailing in the seventh game 3–0 going to the bottom of the sixth inning, the Mets rallied and won that game, too, 5–3.

As of this writing, the Boston Red Sox have not lost a World Series game since, sweeping St. Louis in 2004 and Colorado in 2007.

Shell-Shocked (1988)

The silver screen was the stage for Roy Hobbs and his heroics in *The Natural*. Dodger Stadium was the stage for Kirk Gibson and his mythic heroics in the 1988 World Series.

In a script straight out of Hollywood, the Dodgers were one out away from a 4–3 loss to the Oakland Athletics in the opening game when Gibson put his mark on the game's history.

When the teams were introduced prior to the start of the Series, Kirk Gibson, the National League MVP-in-waiting and the Dodgers' emotional leader, was nowhere to be found.

He had been injured in the National League Championship Series against the Mets and was back in the clubhouse taking a couple of injections to combat the pain in his torn left hamstring and sprained right knee.

All-world closer Dennis Eckersley, as automatic as there was in the late '80s and early '90s, was on to close it out for Oakland. After recording two quick outs, he walked ex-teammate Mike Davis, a .196 hitter in 1988, on a 3–1 pitch.

Beyond the Box Score

Eckersley had walked only 11 batters all season. Two seasons later, in 1990, he would issue a total of three walks.

That brought up Gibson, pinch-hitting and inducing a deafening roar from the crowd inside Dodger Stadium. He limped to the plate dragging his right knee behind him and favoring his left leg. It became immediately clear, when he fouled off a pitch, that even if he hit the ball fair, he might not be able to run all the way to first.

Eckersley quickly blew fastballs by Gibson to run the count to 0–2, but Gibson hung in. Recalling the exquisitely accurate scouting reports, he knew that Eckersley would throw a slider when ahead in the count.

And when he did, Gibson, using an arms-only swing, hit it into the right-field stands, sending fans at Chavez Ravine into bedlam.

The A's, winners of a club-record 104 games and heavily favored to win the World Series, never recovered.

It was "Casey at the Bat," only this time, Casey didn't strike out.

Dodgers in five.

Regarding those fans sent into bedlam: in the tradition of Southern California baseball fans who traditionally arrive late and leave early, *regardless of the score*, the next time you see the clip of Gibson's home run, pay attention to the number of red lights of cars departing the parking lot beyond the pavilion in right field.

Who Needs a Glove (Redux)? (1989)

This episode is about Kevin Mitchell. Yes, *that* Kevin Mitchell, the one who was shot three times in youth gangs and who, as a New York Met, reportedly had to put his uniform pants back on to go out and pinch-hit, prolonging the rally that resulted in Bill Buckner's aforementioned error for the ages.

After the season, the Mets traded Mitchell to San Diego, which in turn dealt him to San Francisco after only three months.

In 1989, having been moved off of third base to the outfield, Mitchell put together an MVP season, the first for a Giants player since 1969. What was most memorable about that heady season was Mitchell's glove—or lack thereof, given that he had not etched a reputation as a dynamic fielder.

On April 26 in St. Louis, Ozzie Smith hit a fly ball toward the left-field corner, hooking foul but still within Mitchell's grasp. Except that Mitchell overran the ball, had to reach back, and caught it barehanded.

Mitchell said, "I was running as hard as I could, and it just came back on me. All I could do was stick up my hand, and there it was."

Through the years, Mitchell was a handful. He is the only player in history to win an MVP Award and play for five teams before he turned 32.

While he was not a model fielder, his uncharacteristic play set the tone for a spectacular season.

Bo Knows Baseball, Too (1989)

He was the uberathlete, in the tradition of the great Jim Thorpe, one of the most gifted and versatile athletes ever to play in professional sports.

Vincent Edward "Bo" Jackson, of Auburn University, won the Heisman Trophy in 1985 running around, through, and over defenders. He could thank blinding speed: 4.12 seconds in the 40-yard dash.

Baseball, though, was his first love. He batted .401 with 17 home runs playing center field as a junior.

The Tampa Bay Buccaneers made him their first pick in the 1986 NFL draft, but Bo didn't like the offer. He did, however, like the offer of the Kansas City Royals, who picked him in the fourth round of the baseball draft—especially after Tampa Bay told him to choose one sport.

He was in the majors that September, after just 53 games in the minors, getting an infield hit in his first at bat and against future Hall of Famer Steve Carlton.

While it was a promising start, a fundamental question lingered among scouts and other baseball people: how would this raw talent ever be able to swing at 90-mile-an-hour fastballs with all that upper-body muscle mass?

Not only did he play well in the highest baseball league on the planet, but also he was selected to start in the outfield on the American League all-star team in 1989 and afterward was named the most valuable player in the game.

In the top of the first inning of that game, played in Anaheim, he made a remarkable catch, saving two runs. More was to come any minute.

Leading off the bottom of the first against the National League's starter, Rick Reuschel, of San Francisco, Jackson hit 448 feet of home run. Bo Jackson went into the record books when Wade Boggs followed him with a long ball of his own, making them the first pair in history to start an All-Star Game with back-to-back home runs.

In addition to his great field work, late in the game, he stole second base, making history in the process. The only other player to hit a home run and steal a base in an All-Star Game: Willie Mays.

Bo Jackson retired with a degenerative hip condition at age 32. Eight seasons in the majors yielded a .250 average with Kansas City, the Chicago White Sox, and the California Angels; four concurrent seasons in the NFL; and the breaking of one bat while checking his swing.

Really.

Rickey Takes a Page from Muhammad Ali (1991)

Just as baseball had never seen the likes of Bo Jackson, who bent or broke the rules, never had it seen the all-around package named Rickey Henderson, another football player in a baseball player's body.

That body began with the Oakland Athletics in 1979 and concluded a *25-year career* in 2003 with the Los Angeles Dodgers. Along the way, he signed the richest contract in major-league history and led the American League in stolen bases when he was 39.

He holds big-league records for stolen bases (1,406), stolen bases in a season (130), walks (2,190), runs (2,295), and leadoff homers (81). That, plus his .401 on-base percentage, made him a first-ballot Hall of Famer in 2009.

In his prime seasons—and there were no shortage of those—when he was reaching base four times out of every 10 plate appearances, he was an absolute pest to opposing pitchers. His crouched stance improved his chances of drawing a walk, and once on base, he was a threat to steal second and put himself in scoring position.

The legendary sportswriter Jim Murray called Rickey Henderson's strike zone "smaller than Hitler's heart."

Henderson played on two World Series winners, the 1989 A's and 1993 Toronto Blue Jays. He was a member of 10 all-star teams. He won a Gold Glove in 1981. He set an all-time one-season stolen-base record with 130 thefts in 1982. In 1990, he became only the fifth leadoff hitter to garner an MVP Award, joining Phil Rizzuto, of the 1950 Yankees; Maury Wills, of the 1962 Dodgers; Zoilo Versalles, of the 1965 Twins; and Pete Rose, of the 1973 Reds.

Not bad for a guy who was born on Christmas Day of 1958 in the backseat of a '57 Oldsmobile on the South Side of Chicago before his mother reached the hospital. She had gone into labor late on Christmas Eve; it was snowing, and she called her husband to come home and drive her. He said no. He was winning big at poker.

From his first breath, Rickey Henderson was always in a rush, but never more so than on May 1, 1991, in a home game at Oakland. In his first at bat, Henderson had walked but then was thrown out attempting to steal by Yankees catcher Matt Nokes. He struck out looking his second time up. Three times was the charm.

At 1:53 P.M. PDT, Rickey stole career base number 939, surpassing Lou Brock's record as the greatest base thief of all time. With Oakland leading 3–2 in the fourth inning, Henderson was on second base after having reached first on an error by shortstop Alvaro Espinosa and then advancing to second on an infield single by Dave Henderson, off of pitcher Tim Leary.

Rickey broke for third and beat Nokes's throw. Lou Brock was in attendance, watching history with Rickey's mom. The game was interrupted. Rickey was given a mike and addressed the crowd, saying, "Lou Brock was the symbol of great base stealing. But today, I am the greatest of all time. Thank you."

When the game resumed and he scored, Nokes shook his hand at home plate.

One day he will officially announce his retirement.

"Jump on My Back, Boys; I'm Carrying You Tonight" (1991)

Kirby Puckett got four hits in his first game in the major leagues, May 8, 1984, at the California Angels, the ninth player ever to collect four hits in his first game.

The problem was that, at 5 feet 9 inches and approximately 220 pounds, he didn't *look* like a major leaguer. He was short and squat but immediately became a Twins fan favorite with his hustle, enthusiastic style of play, and sunny personality. For 12 seasons, he was one of the premier hitters in the game and an outstanding defender, winning a Gold Glove six times.

Beginning in 1986, his second full season in the majors, Kirby Puckett appeared in 10 consecutive All-Star Games. He won the American League batting title in 1989 with a .339 average and batted over .300 eight times. He led the AL or was tied for most hits in a season four times and in 1994 led the league in runs batted in.

Puckett's Twins finished last in 1990. After getting off to a slow start the following season, they put together a 15-game winning streak that propelled them to first place in June. Minnesota won the old Western Division of the American League and defeated Toronto in the American League Championship Series—Kirby Puckett, most valuable player—to advance to the World Series against the Atlanta Braves, another team that had finished last the previous year.

It was one of the most memorable World Series you can name, with three games—including the final two—decided in extra innings. The Twins were trailing three games to two as they played Game 6 at home. Kirby Puckett provided the heroics, backing up in deed his earlier pledge to his teammates that if they were to "jump on [his] back," he would carry them.

In the third inning, he leaped high against the fence in left center to rob Ron Gant of an extra-base hit and snuff out an Atlanta rally.

Then in the 11th inning, Puckett led off against Charlie Leibrandt, who had never relieved in his career. On a 2–1 count, Leibrandt hung a changeup and Puckett hit it into the seats in left center field to get the Twins even at three games and force Game 7. He became the ninth player to end a World Series game with a home run.

The following night, in one of best games in the history of the World Series, the Twins scored in the 10th inning to win 1–0 and capture their first world championship since 1987.

Sid Bream Had Talents, Speed Not Being One of Them (1992)

Sid Bream came up through the Los Angeles Dodgers system with a reputation as a power-hitting first baseman. He could also hit for average: witness a career .329 average. He arrived in 1983.

Two years later, he was dealt to a terrible Pittsburgh team for former batting champion Bill Madlock. Bream flourished with the Pirates until injuries intervened. After solid seasons in 1987 and 1988, Bream underwent three knee operations, including a reconstruction. The knee never fully healed. What speed he had was now gone.

In 1991, Bream was on an Atlanta team that became the first in National League history to go from last place to first place in the same season.

That fall, and the one to follow, he and the Braves faced Bream's former club, the Pirates, in the National League Championship Series.

In '91, Bream tormented his former club, batting .300 in seven games as the Braves advanced to an eventual seven-game loss to Minnesota in the World Series.

The following year, the Pirates led the seventh and deciding NLCS game 2–0 in Atlanta. If they could hold off the Braves, they would advance to their first World Series since 1979.

A walk to Bream loaded the bases with no one out.

A sacrifice fly made it 2–1. Dave Justice was on third, Bream was on second, and Damon Berryhill, who had walked to reload the bases, was on first.

Atlanta called on the last man on its bench to pinch-hit, Francisco Cabrera.

The stakes were only these: get a hit, your team goes to the World Series; make an out, the opposition Pirates go.

Facing Pirates closer Stan Belinda, Cabrera grounded a single past shortstop into left field. Justice scored from third to tie it.

Years later, Andy Van Slyke, who was playing center field that night for Pittsburgh, told me that he yelled at Bonds to play up in left field, to take some steps closer to the infield in anticipation of a possible play at the plate. Bonds refused. There's a saying in baseball, "The ball will find you." Sure enough, Cabrera's single found Bonds. Had he been playing up, his chances of throwing out the slow-footed Bream at the plate would have increased exponentially. As my fabulous mother, Nora, would have said, "Thickhead!"

Bream, who was one of the slowest men in baseball and ran as if he were carrying a piano on his back, chugged around third. Barry Bonds, in what would be his final game as a Pirate, charged the ball and threw home.

Mike Lavalliere, the Pittsburgh catcher, caught the ball and lunged toward the sliding Bream.

Safe!

The Braves, starting with Justice waiting for him at the plate, piled out of the dugout and on top of Bream as Atlanta returned to the World Series.

To this day and for countless days to follow in Atlanta, Sid Bream is remembered for The Slide.

Fame was fleeting for Francisco Cabrera. He was gone from the major leagues after the following season.

And the Pittsburgh Pirates have not had a winning season, much less a postseason appearance, since 1992.

An eternal question is what would have happened if that game had been played with the normal complement of four umpires. In the first inning, home-plate umpire John McSherry—who began his umpiring career umpiring in my Little League in the Bronx, the University Heights Little League—left the game with chest pains. That forced first-base ump Randy Marsh to slide down the line and call balls and strikes. In the decisive ninth inning, Pirates closer Stan Belinda threw a number of close pitches that were called balls instead of strikes. Many in baseball believe he was "squeezed" by Marsh behind the plate. Pirates fans have wondered for years how that ninth inning might have transpired, with their club trying to protect a 2–0 lead as the World Series beckoned, had John McSherry not been forced to leave.

Joe Carter (1993)

It was the bottom of the ninth inning in Toronto, Game 6 of the World Series, October 23, 1993.

Philadelphia led the game 6–5 but trailed in the Series three games to two. The Blue Jays had two runners on base, with one out.

Philadelphia manager Jim Fregosi removed Roger Mason, pitching effectively, and replaced him with his closer, Mitch Williams, not nicknamed "the Wild Thing" for nothing, trying to force a seventh and deciding game.

At bat was one of the game's trustiest run producers, Joe Carter, hitless in his four career trips to the plate against Williams but one of only a dozen players to have at least 12 consecutive seasons with 20 or more home runs.

The other 11 players to rack up 12 consecutive seasons with 20 or more home runs are all in the Hall of Fame: Hank Aaron (20); Babe Ruth and Willie Mays (16); Eddie Mathews and Mike Schmidt (14); Reggie Jackson, Willie Stargell, and Billy Williams (13); Jimmie Foxx, Lou Gehrig, and Frank Robinson (12).

Williams quickly threw two pitches out of the strike zone. The next two were strikes.

The all-time stolen-base leader, Rickey Henderson, was at second base representing the potential tying run, and his mere presence is credited with diverting Williams's full attention from Carter. The next pitch was down and in, in Carter's happy zone, just where he liked it. He put a good swing on it and hit it deep to left. Phillies left fielder Pete Incaviglia ran to the wall, turned his back, and stopped to watch it sail into the stands.

Joe Carter jumped up and down as he circled the bases, making sure he touched every base, celebrating the kind of moment most people live out only in dreamland.

It was pandemonium in the SkyDome as the Jays retained their world champion status, the first team to do so since the 1977–78 New York Yankees.

The ball landed no more than 60 feet away from me in the auxiliary press box. Ever hear massive fireworks explode indoors? What did you say?

Carter's famous home-run ball was returned to him that night, courtesy of retiring bullpen coach John Sullivan, and Joe Carter took his place beside Bill Mazeroski as the ninth-inning World Series heroes of all time, who hit a home run that will travel through baseball history forever.

Carter presented the climactic legendary home-run ball that confirmed his reservation in baseball history to his wife, Diana. Here's why: As a minor leaguer in the Chicago Cubs system, he once had to sell his cowboy boots, which Diana had given him, for $40 so they could eat. He was playing in Midland, Texas, making $600 a month, and Diana was pregnant with their first child. The $40 had to last them several days.

At Midland, when someone from the home team homered, the fans had a ritual of passing a hat around, throwing money into it, and giving it to the player who homered. On the morning of a day when Joe Carter's parents were expected for a visit, he went to the refrigerator to see what he could scrounge up for dinner. There was nothing there but a half loaf of bread, some butter, and milk.

Carter turned to Diana and said he had to hit a home run that night so they could pass the hat around for him. Sure enough, Carter hit one out. They passed the hat around and collected $54.00. The grocery bill was $54.10.

He had the extra dime for the best meal they ate that year.

CHAPTER 11
Defining and Climbing the Standings

◆◆◆◆◆◆◆◆◆◆◆◆◆◆◆◆◆◆◆◆◆◆◆◆

Major League Baseball has 30 clubs: 16 in the National League, 14 in the American. Each league has three geographic divisions: East, Central, and West. The National League was founded in 1876, the American in 1901. That is why the NL is commonly referred to as the "senior circuit."

Until 1997, the only times the teams in one league would play the other were during spring training and in the World Series. That year, interleague play began. On two occasions—in May and June—teams from the National League play American League teams, with the home team determining the rules (DH or no DH) for each game.

To determine each team's status within its league, take a look on the next spread at the sample set of standings from early in the season. The four columns show wins, losses, winning percentage, and number of games back.

Losses are the most critical factor in determining standings. Wins can always be made up. The standings are established by losses and games played. Take the American East from our sample standings. Toronto is in first place, with Boston in second, though the two teams have the same number of losses, 12. The Blue Jays are in first place by virtue of their having played two more games, both of which they have won. Those wins have given the Jays a higher winning percentage than Boston's.

	W	L	PCT	GB
American League				
East				
Toronto Blue Jays	23	12	.657	—
Boston Red Sox	21	12	.636	1.0
New York Yankees	15	17	.469	6.5
Tampa Bay Rays	15	19	.441	7.5
Baltimore Orioles	14	19	.424	8.0
Central				
Detroit Tigers	17	14	.548	—
Kansas City Royals	18	15	.545	—
Minnesota Twins	16	17	.485	2.0
Chicago White Sox	15	17	.469	2.5
Cleveland Indians	12	22	.353	6.5
West				
Texas Rangers	18	14	.563	—
Los Angeles Angels	16	15	.516	1.5
Seattle Mariners	16	17	.485	2.5
Oakland Athletics	12	18	.400	5.0

As Yogi would have put it, once a game is lost, it's lost. Here's something else Yogiesque: every game is a half game.

Example: Tonight, if Toronto is not scheduled to play and Boston is, and the Red Sox win their game, the Sox gain a half game on the Jays. They'd now be 22–12. If, on the next night, Toronto again was off and the Red Sox played and won, they would become 23–12 and move into a first-place tie with the Jays.

Now let's figure out why Toronto leads Tampa Bay by 7½ (7.5) games. The Jays are 23–12. That's 35 games played. Tampa Bay is 15–19, which equals 34 games. If I didn't know the Jays were 7½ games behind and needed to figure that out, I'd look at the difference in the

	W	L	PCT	GB
National League				
East				
New York Mets	18	14	.563	—
Philadelphia Phillies	16	14	.533	1.0
Florida Marlins	17	16	.515	1.5
Atlanta Braves	16	17	.485	2.5
Washington Nationals	10	21	.323	7.5
Central				
St. Louis Cardinals	20	13	.606	—
Cincinnati Reds	19	14	.576	1.0
Milwaukee Brewers	19	14	.576	1.0
Chicago Cubs	18	14	.563	1.5
Houston Astros	14	18	.438	5.5
Pittsburgh Pirates	13	19	.406	6.5
West				
Los Angeles Dodgers	22	12	.647	—
San Francisco Giants	18	14	.563	3.0
Colorado Rockies	13	18	.419	7.5
San Diego Padres	13	20	.394	8.5
Arizona Diamondbacks	13	21	.382	9.0

win column. Toronto has 23, versus Tampa Bay's 15. That's a difference of 8.

Now look at the loss column. Toronto has 12, versus Tampa Bay's 19, a difference of 7.

The difference in the standings between Toronto and Tampa Bay is the midpoint of those two figures. The difference between 8 in the win column and 7 in the loss column yields 7.5 games behind.

Now let's look at the American League Central. If Detroit and Kansas City each had 17 wins and 14 losses, they would be in what is commonly called in baseball a "flat-footed tie." However, in this case, Detroit has 17 wins and 14 losses, while Kansas City has 18 wins and 15 losses. Detroit has one fewer win but also one fewer loss, because the Tigers have played two fewer games. Here, the determining factor is winning percentage, which is based on 1.000 (i.e., a team with a record of 10 wins and 0 losses would have a winning percentage of 1.000; conversely, a team that had no wins and 10 losses would have a winning percentage of .000). Since Detroit's record is three percentage points higher than Kansas City's, Detroit is awarded first place in what is commonly called a "virtual tie."

The Evolution of the World Series

The origins of baseball remain in doubt. What is certain is that, despite being credited with doing so, Abner Doubleday did *not* invent the game in Cooperstown. There were leagues and associations of baseball teams that played as far back as the 1840s.

The National Association (later, the National League) was formed in 1876, and the American Association was formed six years later. For the ensuing six-year period, from 1884 through 1890, the winners in each met in the postseason, a concept never tried before. The American Association died in 1891, with four of its teams being absorbed by the National League.

The American Association was succeeded by the formation of the American League in 1901. The National League did not take lightly to the new competition and waged war by raiding players. Two years later, in 1903, the leagues announced not only a truce but also a series of games to be played against each other after the conclusion of the regular season.

Arranged by the owners and not by the leagues, the inaugural contest matched Pittsburgh, of the National League, against Boston, of the American League. Boston won the best-of-nine series, five games to three, behind the pitching of Bill Dineen and Cy Young (who never won a Cy Young award).

The following year was to have matched the AL's Boston Americans, forebears of the Red Sox, against the New York Giants in the NL. It didn't, because the owner of the Giants refused to put his team on the field, contending that his league was the only true major league. In the absence of a commissioner or governing body, no one was empowered to do anything about it. So, when you look up the list of World Series winners and losers, you see this entry next to the year 1904: No series.

After negotiations, the Series returned for 1905, with the Giants defeating the Philadelphia Athletics four games to one. For the next 89 years, the World Series was played without interruption, until September 14, 1994, when major-league owners called it off due to the strike that had begun the month before.

The modern World Series has been played as a best-of-seven series except in 1903, and in 1919 through 1921, when the victor was determined through a best-of-nine play-off.

The History of Divisional Play

Man, I wish I could have majored in this in college, ya know?

Through the 1968 season, the American and National League standings were one listing apiece with 10 teams each. If a team finished anywhere from first to fifth in its league, it was said to be in the "first division." That fall, each league expanded by two teams—the American to Kansas City and Seattle, the National to Montreal and San Diego. Each league, for the first time, split into divisions, East and West, with six clubs apiece.

Little-known fact: when the National League drew up its divisions, it originally placed the St. Louis Cardinals in the West and the Atlanta Braves in the East. Made sense, right? With the Cards' chief rival, the Cubs, in the East along with the big-market teams in New York and Philadelphia, Gussie Busch, the Cards' owner, thought otherwise. Being one of the most influential owners in baseball, he persuaded his peers to place his team in the East.

The two-division structure remained in place until late 1992 when the National League expanded to South Florida and Denver with the birth of the Florida Marlins and Colorado Rockies, to begin play in 1993. Florida was added to the East, Colorado to the West.

Five years later, in 1997, each league expanded by one team apiece for the following season—this time, to Tampa–St. Pete and Phoenix. The American League added the Tampa Bay Devil Rays, matched in the National by the Arizona Diamondbacks. A problem with this expansion was that it gave each league 15 teams, an odd number.

To remedy this situation, Bud Selig proposed that his team, the Milwaukee Brewers, switch from the American League to the National. That is why, to this day, there are 16 teams in the National League and 14 in the American.

The Modern Postseason Explained

If you finish first in your division, you make the play-offs. There are six of those slots available overall—three in each league in the East, Central, and West divisions.

The problem of having an odd number of teams in a play-off bracket is resolved by the inclusion of the wild-card team. That team is the one with the best record in its league that did not finish first in its division. These two wild cards—one in each league—get in regardless of the divisions in which they play.

The first round of the play-offs in each league, the Divisional Series, is a best-of-five match. The team with the best overall regular-season record gets the top seed and home-field advantage. It hosts the first two games and will host the fifth and deciding game, if necessary. The team with the second-best record is accorded the same courtesy.

Typically, the wild-card team plays the team with the best overall record; however, the wild card is forbidden from playing a team in its own division in the opening series. Here's why: Say the season ended with the standings similar to the rankings presented at the beginning of this chapter, and the Dodgers won the NL West while the Giants went on to become the wild card. It would be unfair if the Giants could advance to the league championship over a team that had a better record than they did without at least facing elimination in another series first. Therefore, if the wild card and the best overall team in the league both hail from the same division, the wild-card team will play the team with the second-best record.

The first team to win three games advances to the next round, the League Championship Series. This is a best-of-seven series. Note that the teams with the best record of baseball's "final four" are not always granted home-field advantage. Should the wild-card team survive and have a better record than the other qualifying team, which won its division, the division champion still gets the advantage and hosts the first two games and the last two, if necessary.

Finally, the survivor from the NL meets its counterpart from the AL in a best-of-seven World Series. In the 2009 Series, home-field advantage—the opportunity to host the maximum four home games—went to the American League because the AL won that summer's All-Star Game, which is the way home-field advantage in the World Series has been decided since 2003.

Beyond the Box Score

Since 1933, the All-Star Game has matched the best players in the American League against those in the National League in an exhibition game. After the 2002 All-Star Game ended in a tie (the game was called when both teams ran out of pitchers, as their respective managers were trying to get everyone in the game), MLB was prompted to raise the stakes (and the ratings) by making the game "count" and having both teams play for their league's play-off advantage. The American League has won home-field advantage in each contest since, through the 2009 season.

Today's October Baseball

Baseball purists like myself loved the fact that baseball was the last remaining sport in which finishing first mattered through the course of six months and 162 games.

Introducing the wild card diminished the significance of winning a divisional championship. Still, in the interest of complete candor, I admit that I have grudgingly come to accept the change. The best-of-five format in the Divisional Series has given us play-offs as intense and compelling as any others in professional sports.

Every year from 2002 through 2007, at least one wild-card team advanced to the World Series. The 2002 World Series, between the Anaheim Angels and San Francisco Giants, featured two wild-card teams, the only time that has happened. Both the 2003 and 2004 World Series winners also started their path through October as wild cards.

Unfortunately, there have been occasions when a team failed to make the play-offs despite having a better record than another team in the league that made the play-offs by winning its division.

Since the imposition of the second tier of play-offs in 1995, it has happened three times in the American League. Thirteen is the corresponding number in the National League, four of which occasions were in 2008. The Los Angeles Dodgers won the West and went to the play-offs with a worse record than New York, Houston, St. Louis, and Florida.

There may be sufficient sentiment to eventually extend the opening-round Divisional Series from five games to seven.

CHAPTER 12

Momentous Moments— the Wild-Card Era (1994–Present)

On September 9, 1993, by a margin of 27 to 1, major-league owners voted to realign each league into a three-division format, adding a Central division to join the East and West.

As noted previously, three divisions naturally makes for three division winners, and that does not compute for postseason play. The remedy was instituting a wild-card team, to yield an even four contenders.

The plan was for the new format to debut in 1994. However, the longest work stoppage in American professional sports history postponed the crowning of baseball's first wild-card teams until the year thereafter.

Our Nuclear Winter (1994–95)

Eight work stoppages in 22 years: count 'em. I have covered six as a reporter. Talk about depressing. Among them all, the work stoppage of 1994 takes the cake.

On September 14, 1994, a little more than a month after play was halted, commissioner Bud Selig walked to the podium at the Inter-

Continental Hotel in Manhattan and announced that the World Series had been canceled.

Let's just put that in perspective: the World Series had been played through two World Wars, conflicts in Korea and Vietnam, the Depression, and recessions, in good times and in bad.

Now let's take a depressing minute to put the moments of labor unrest into perspective:

Strike One—1972

The first full-scale strike in MLB history took place when players staged a collective 86-game, 13-day walkout at the end of spring training to demand an increase in pension payments. After 10 days, team owners granted the players the pension increases as well as the right to arbitrate salary disputes—a major factor behind the rise in player salaries after 1972.

The strike wiped out the first week of the regular season. Baseball designated April 15 as opening day and forgot about makeups. As a result, not every team missed playing the same number of games during the strike. That it was a flawed strategy became evident as the Detroit Tigers beat out the Boston Red Sox, even though the two teams had the same number of losses, by virtue of Detroit's having played one more game on the schedule.

Lockout—1973

The first lockout by ownership in Major League Baseball history was over salary arbitration and lasted seven days in spring training.

Lockout—1976

Disagreements over free agency caused a 17-day spring-training lockout.

Strike Two—1980

Free-agency disputes again affected spring training, this time for one week.

Strike Three—1981

On June 11, players struck after owners proposed a system for compensating clubs that had lost players to free agency. The walkout lasted 712 games and cost the players $30 million in unpaid salaries, while the owners claimed $116 million in lost revenue. The 50-day strike was settled by a compromise that gave the owners a victory on the issue of free-agent compensation but allowed the players to avoid a proposed cap on salaries. The strike was settled July 31 with the announcement that the season would resume with the All-Star Game in Cleveland on August 9.

Three days earlier, the owners decided to split the season into halves, the first time it had done so since 1892. That format was flawed, too. It prevented the Cincinnati Reds and St. Louis Cardinals from making the play-offs, despite their having the two best full-season records in the National League. Meanwhile, in the American League, the Kansas City Royals somehow qualified for the postseason with a cumulative season's record of 50–53.

Strike Four—1985

In 1985, skyrocketing player salaries led owners to demand a salary cap and an increase in the number of years' experience that a player needed in order to qualify for salary arbitration. The strike began on August 6 and ended just two days later—with 25 games lost—when the dispute was resolved. The lost games were rescheduled. The owners won an increase in the minimum experience for salary arbitration from two years to three, while the players avoided a salary cap and were given an increase in their pensions.

Collusion—1985–87

The clubs were found guilty of collusion for "fixing" the markets for the free-agent classes of 1985–87. Those unlawful practices reinforced the union's distrust of the clubs. No work stoppage coincided with that practice—a $280 million settlement soothed the wronged players—but the expiration of the labor agreement of 1985 set the stage for the spring-training lockout of 1990.

So distasteful and provocative were the collusion episodes that, in late 1989, new commissioner Fay Vincent dismissed Barry Rona, the clubs' lead negotiator, on the eve of the first collective-bargaining session because he recognized the union's overriding distrust. Even with Rona gone and the finished product little more than an extension of the status quo, a negotiated agreement took weeks.

Lockout—1990

Salary-arbitration and salary-cap issues delayed spring training for 32 days and postponed the start of the regular season.

Strike Five—1994–95

The longest labor stoppage in U.S. professional sports history to that point began August 12, 1994, and ended in a courtroom March 31, 1995, when MLB owners decided to allow striking players to return to work rather than lock them out and field teams of replacement players. The walkout had forced the cancellation of 920 games and, for the first time in 90 years, the World Series, the most conspicuous victim.

Beyond the Box Score

The 1994–95 strike wasn't the most acrimonious of the eight work stoppages that have stained and strained the game since the players' union demonstrated its resolve in 1972.

That distinction goes to the strike in 1981, which changed how the clubs, the public, and the players themselves viewed the professional athlete. The '81 strike was nasty, made so in large part by the decision of the clubs to bring in Ray Grebey, a hired gun, as their negotiator opposite Marvin Miller, the union's founding executive director and tower of strength.

The '94 strike, though, was the longest and was the most damaging as well with the elimination of the World Series, one of the guideposts of American sporting life. In addition, some stellar regular-season performances—the runs at division championships by the Yankees and Montreal Expos, Matt Williams's pursuit of the single-season home-run record (he had 43 when play was halted), and Tony Gwynn's run at .400 (he was batting .394)—were ended prematurely.

The money lost by both sides and by people and businesses on the baseball periphery was incalculable. Some fans and businesses never returned.

The underlying issue in 1994 was the same as it was in 1981: the desire of clubs to restrict players' salaries. In 1981, the owners thought "taxing" a club for signing a free agent would make their peers reluctant to sign these players, limiting salaries. The convoluted structure—indirect compensation involving selections in the ensuing amateur draft of high school and college players—didn't accomplish the stated objectives.

In 1994, clubs planned to let the collective-bargaining agreement with the players' union lapse and then impose a salary cap. The union struck before the contract expired.

The players subsequently were ordered back to work after 234 days by eventual supreme court justice Sonya Sotomayor, who

(continued)

issued an injunction on March 31, 1995, ordering governance of the game under terms of the expired labor agreement. Three days later, the day before the new season was scheduled to start, the strike was finally over. Sotomayor scolded the owners for what she deemed unfair labor practices and urged lawyers for striking players and the owners to salvage the 1995 season, reach a new labor agreement, and change their attitudes. The strike, she said, had "placed the entire of collective bargaining on trial."

After play resumed, the *Philadelphia Inquirer* lauded Judge Sotomayor, comparing her to Joe DiMaggio, Ted Williams, Jackie Robinson, and Willie Mays. The *Chicago Sun-Times* called her "one of the most inspiring figures in the history of sport."

Cal 2,132 Saves Baseball (1995)

Shell-shocked, baseball returned with a 144-game season in 1995. The bitterness among those who loved the game or who had the immense good fortune to be in it was palpable.

Cue the savior.

Cal Ripken Jr. was a reluctant hero, believing in a day's work for a day's pay and that what he did as the shortstop for the Baltimore Orioles was no different from what you and I do. His attitude was stunningly simple: "I go out to play, period, because that's what I should do; that's what I was taught when I was growing up."

Play he did, beginning May 30, 1982, his rookie season. To put the streak in perspective, consider that when it started, the Dow Jones average was 819.54.

Playing shortstop, a high-traffic position that takes its toll on the body, Ripken was expected to surpass the record of 2,131 consecutive games played by Lou Gehrig, the Yankees' "Iron Horse," during the 1994 season.

The strike to end all strikes postponed the climax of the chase.

Unlike Hank Aaron's chase of Babe Ruth's home-run record and Pete Rose's race to Ty Cobb's all-time hits mark, Ripken didn't have the pressure of the countdown at every at bat.

Basically, he just had to show up. In doing so, he redefined how shortstop was played in the major leagues, making it safe for big men like him at six foot four to serve there.

On September 6, 1995, against the California Angels in Baltimore, Cal Ripken became the new "Iron Man." He even hit a home run in the fourth inning to give the Orioles the lead at Camden Yards. So, when the Angels went down without scoring in the fifth inning, it was an official game. Play was halted for 22 minutes as Ripken lapped the stands of the delirious ballpark.

The streak continued into 1998. It came to an end at 2,632 games on September 20, the date of the Orioles' last home game for the season, and its conclusion was easy to detect. He was nowhere to be seen on the field while Baltimore took batting practice before that game.

The opposing New York Yankees realized Ripken wouldn't be playing for the first time in 16 seasons. They lined the top step of the dugout and applauded; Ripken saluted them with a wave of his cap before returning to the bench.

The Streak, which deserves capitalization, was an astonishing accomplishment that set Cal Ripken Jr. apart for his simple approach that he should be ready to play every day. It earned for him the lasting respect of fans everywhere, men and women who were expected to be on the job every day in their own professions.

He helped heal the wounds.

A savior.

Griffey's Dash (1995)

It was a season when he missed 73 games, half the season, after fracturing both bones in his left wrist—an injury he suffered while making a spectacular catch on Kevin Bass in center field May 26, 1995, against Baltimore. His Seattle Mariners went 36–37 until he returned August 15. But this was about his legs, not his hands.

With Ken Griffey Jr. absent, the Mariners were 12½ games out of first place. Despite playing with a four-inch metal plate and seven screws attached to his wrist, he hit 10 home runs in the 45 games he played in during the second half of the season, but still finished with a career-low .258 average with 17 homers and 42 runs batted in. The Mariners ended the regular season tied with the California Angels for first place in the American League West. A one-game play-off would determine who would advance to the postseason.

With Randy Johnson pitching a complete-game victory, Seattle played in October for the first time in a franchise history dating to its birth in 1977. The Yankees awaited in a best-of-five Division Series.

New York won both games in New York, New York, with the second duel lasting 15 innings. Seattle won the next two, including wiping out a 5–0 New York lead in the first inning of game four.

Every baseball demigod needs the Defining Moment.

Mays had the catch off Vic Wertz. Hank Aaron had number 715 off Al Downing. Ken Griffey Jr. had The Run.

Junior was on first base in the bottom of the 11th inning in the fifth and deciding game. The Yankees were leading 5–4. Joey Cora was on third, having been sent there by a hard-hit single to center by Griffey. Edgar Martinez drove a ball into the left-field corner. Cora scored easily to tie the game.

And now here came Griffey, running at breakneck speed, determined to score the winning run. At that moment, there was no faster man on the planet.

Gerald Williams picked up the ball in left field and relayed it to shortstop Tony Fernandez, whose throw home arrived after Griffey slid in safely, giving the Mariners a 6–5 win and a trip to the ALCS.

Tony Fernandez was the last Yankees shortstop before Derek Jeter.

Nobody cared that Griffey batted only .258 with 17 homers and 42 RBIs during the season. They were a memory when he awakened to hit five home runs in the five games against the Yankees, drove in seven, and hit .391.

Let the celebrating begin!

A Magic Trick (1996)

A 12-year-old boy from Old Tappan, New Jersey, went to Yankee Stadium for the opening game of the American League Divisional Series against Baltimore.

Chances are Jeffrey Maier didn't drive.

But he did drive the Orioles nuts.

On October 9, 1996, Baltimore led 4–3 in the bottom of the eighth inning. The Yankees' Derek Jeter, playing his first full season, lifted a fly ball off of Orioles reliever Armando Benitez deep to right field.

Outfielder Tony Tarasco retreated to the wall, put his back up against it, raised his glove to make the catch, and . . .

Poof, it was gone.

Tarasco said he thought that he was at the circus, that someone had made the ball just disappear.

That's because Maier, having run out of his seat and stationed himself directly above Tarasco, reached over the fence separating the right-field stands from the field of play and deflected the ball with his mitt.

Jeter started running around the bases, assuming it was a home run. Tarasco immediately appealed to Richie Phillips, the umpire down the right-field line.

In the postseason, two extra umpires are added to the crew, one on each of the foul lines in the outfield.

Phillips signaled home run.

The Orioles went nuts.

It was clearly a case of fan interference, and Phillips would have been within his rights to nullify Jeter's home run and declare it an out, putout 9.

Instead, it went down as one of the worst umpiring calls in history, straight into the Denkinger Hall of Fame of Blown Calls.

Replays from every conceivable angle clearly showed that the 12-year-old boy from New Jersey interfered with play.

Mariano Rivera pitched two scoreless innings, and the Yankees eventually won 5–4 in 11 innings on Bernie Williams's home run off of Randy Myers.

New York, in its constant, voracious search for the next celebrity and its reservoir of 15 minutes of fame, turned its lonely eyes to Jeffrey Maier.

 Beyond the Box Score — Richie Phillips, now one of seven umpire supervisors for Major League Baseball, later admitted he made the wrong call, but American League president Gene Budig denied Baltimore's protest.

There was a news conference, a fight among the three network morning shows won by "Good Morning America," an appearance on "Regis and Kathie Lee," and the *New York Daily News*'s giving the Maier family tickets for Game 2—right behind the Yankees dugout—in exchange for documenting A Day in the Life of Jeffrey Maier.

The Orioles lost the series and, after one more year in the play-offs, lost their way. Davey Johnson, who was the manager that day and was ejected in the subsequent argument and fired a year later under mysterious circumstances, believes he could still be in Baltimore were it not for that play. Jeffrey Maier became a symbol of the futility from which the Orioles have yet to recover. Maier grew up to attend Wesleyan University in Connecticut, where he played the outfield and third base and where he broke the school record for hits, batting .375.

There was even talk of his being drafted. But no Division Three school had had a player drafted since 1965, nor had one produced a major-league player since 1916.

Good thing for Maier. Armando Benitez was waiting. He said he hoped Maier made it to the major leagues, "just so I can drill him—I'd like to get one shot at him."

In choosing Wesleyan, Jeffrey Maier passed up an opportunity to attend Johns Hopkins University, in Maryland. He explained, "I was like, 'I can't do that.' It would've been nuts for me to go down there." Instead, Maryland came to him: a fellow student from suburban Baltimore produced a short film for her senior thesis with the engaging title "I Hate Jeffrey Maier." It concerns an Orioles fan who attends the same college as Maier and who confronts his own repressed anger over The Play. Maier himself makes a cameo at the end.

Three Weeks Before the Fire Sale (1997)

How many times as a kid did you imagine batting in the bottom of the ninth inning of the seventh game of the World Series with a chance to win it?

It gets even better if the game's in extra innings.

On the night of Sunday, October 26, 1997, the Florida Marlins, playing at home in their first World Series in just their fifth season of existence, were tied 2–2 with Cleveland. The Indians, playing in their second World Series in three years, were three outs away from their first world championship since 1948, when closer Jose Mesa gave up the tying run in the bottom of the ninth inning.

In the home 11th inning, the bases were loaded with two outs and 22-year-old shortstop Edgar Renteria, in his second season, at the plate. Facing Charles Nagy, Renteria bounced a ground ball off the pitcher's glove into center field for the hit that scored Craig Counsell from third base to win the World Series.

The joy was short lived.

Team owner Wayne Huizenga, arbitrarily claiming the club was swimming in an ocean of red ink, ordered general manager Dave Dombrowski to dismantle the championship team by whatever means necessary.

Just five days later, Moises Alou, who had hit three homers and driven in nine runs in the World Series and could have been named its MVP, was traded to the Houston Astros for an inequitable return.

Over the winter, most of the former Florida players were scattered across baseball. The following season, the Florida Marlins won 54 games and lost 108, becoming the first championship team to lose 100 or more games the following season.

Mark McGwire (1998), Sammy Sosa (1998), Barry Bonds (2001)

Truly, I choose to not write thoughtful imagery regarding these players due to allegations that all three adulterated the game with performance-enhancing drugs.

He Didn't Slide Because Why? (2001)

A blown relay yielded a play that the A's and their fans would like to sweep away from their collective memories.

The Oakland Athletics began the best-of-five American League Division Series against the Yankees by winning the first two games in New York. They went for the three-game sweep at home but trailed 1–0 on catcher Jorge Posada's home run off of Barry Zito in the fifth inning.

In the Oakland seventh inning, Jeremy Giambi was on first base when Terrence Long laced a Mike Mussina pitch down the right-field line and into the corner. As Giambi raced around the bases with the apparent tying run, Shane Spencer retrieved the ball but made a bad throw, eluding the cutoff man, throwing it over his head. The ball bounced halfway between first base and home plate.

Out of nowhere, Yankees shortstop Derek Jeter appeared, having run across the infield toward the first-base line. He intercepted the ball and made a backhand flip to Posada, who tagged out the oncoming Giambi (*who inexplicably did not slide*).

The Yankees won that game, 1–0, and the next two, en route to their fifth World Series appearance in six years.

Though Jeter was deified for his heads-up play and Giambi was skewered for coming in standing up, in truth, Giambi probably would have been out even if Jeter had let the ball go through and Giambi had slid.

Still, in answer to what Jeter was doing even being there, coach Don Zimmer said the Yankees practice that play in spring training.

Tino, Brosius, and the Birth of Mr. November (2001)

There have been 104 World Series as of this writing.

None may have been more emotional than the one that unfolded in 2001 against the backdrop of the recent events of September 11.

The Arizona Diamondbacks had mortgaged their financial future to make a championship run in just their fourth year of existence, committing tens of millions in contracts for Randy Johnson, Curt Schilling, Matt Williams, and Steve Finley.

The New York Yankees, seeking their fourth consecutive world championship, for the first time received the seeming support of baseball fans across the country, who were sympathetic at the plight of the city in the wake of the terrorist attacks. The consequent postponement of games following the tragedy delayed the start of the World Series until October 27, the latest date ever.

Schilling and Johnson won the first two games easily in Phoenix by an aggregate score of 13–1. As the Series moved to the Bronx on Halloween, an emotional crowd welcomed President Bush, with chants of "U-S-A, U-S-A." He became the first president to throw out the first pitch in a World Series game since Dwight Eisenhower in 1956, before Roger Clemens and the Yanks won 2–1.

Schilling returned to the mound in Game 4 and was brilliant once again, leaving after seven innings with a 3–1 lead. Byung-Hyun Kim, the Arizona closer who gave up only 58 hits during the regular season in 98 innings with 113 strikeouts, was brought on for the two-inning save. Kim thereby became the first Korean-born player in the World Series.

With two outs in the ninth inning and Paul O'Neill on base, Tino Martinez hit Kim's first pitch over the wall in right center field to tie the game 3–3.

In the 12th inning, well after the clock struck midnight, with Kim still on the mound, Derek Jeter homered to right field to give the Yankees a 2–1 victory to square the Series at two games apiece.

Jeter had barely touched home plate when the video board spelled out "Mr. November" in honor of his being the first player to hit a home run in that month.

Later that night in Game 5, again Arizona had a lead, 2–0, and again Byung-Hyun Kim was called on in the ninth inning to protect it. Jorge Posada's leadoff double brought the potential tying run to the plate. Kim retired the next two batters, sending third baseman Scott Brosius to the plate.

For the second straight night, again with two outs, the big blast came through. Brosius homered into the left-field stands at a delirious Yankee Stadium to tie the game and again force extra innings. And again, the Yankees won the game in 12 innings, this time on Alfonso Soriano's base hit, scoring Chuck Knoblauch.

New York now led the Series three games to two, thanks to a pair of the most emotional victories in World Series history.

It's Not How Far It Goes (2001)

If the Arizona Diamondbacks were demoralized in Phoenix after returning from the emotional losses in New York, you'd have never known it.

They stayed alive behind Randy Johnson, crushing the Yankees in Game 6, 15–2, and setting up a climactic seventh game pitting Curt Schilling against Roger Clemens. In the eighth inning, Alfonso Soriano hit an 0–2 Schilling pitch off his shoe tops and into the left-field stands to give New York a 2–1 lead. Mariano Rivera, the greatest closer in postseason history, entered the game in the bottom of the eighth inning for an unaccustomed two-inning save.

Rivera continued his brilliant pitching, striking out the side, and appeared to be on his way to converting his 24th consecutive save opportunity. His lifetime postseason ERA at that point: 0.70.

Then, the unthinkable happened in the ninth.

The failed strategy of calling on their closer instead of the traditional setup man in the eighth inning would haunt the Yankees again three years later in the 2004 ALCS against Boston.

Poor defensive play by the Yankees was instrumental in giving Arizona the run they needed to tie the game. Now Luis Gonzalez, who had slugged 57 home runs during the season and was beloved in the local community as its most popular player, batted against Rivera with the bases loaded and one out. Yankees manager Joe Torre fatefully decided to bring his infield in for a potential play at the plate.

On an 0–1 pitch, Gonzalez hit a bloop single over second base that barely reached the outfield grass, scoring Jay Bell with the winning run.

Randy Johnson, who had won Game 6 throwing 104 pitches, had caused gasps in the crowd when he emerged from the dugout to go to the bullpen to warm up for possible relief duty. He ended up pitching one and one-third innings, allowing no hits and striking out one batter and being credited with wins in games six and seven.

The gamble to significantly expand payroll paid dividends for the Diamondbacks. They outscored the Yankees 37–14, holding them to a .183 composite average, and, in their fourth year, became the fastest expansion team to win a World Series, only the third Series in which the home team won every game.

 Beyond the Box Score

Prior to Gonzalez's batting, Craig Counsell was hit by a pitch to load the bases. He had scored the winning run on Edgar Renteria's Series-ending hit for Florida four years prior. This was the third World Series Game 7 to end on a hit with the bases loaded in the bottom of the final inning—1991 was the other—and Counsell was involved in two of them.

Jeffrey Maier Redux (2003)

The Chicago Cubs stood five outs away from their first World Series appearance since shortly after the armistice with Germany and Japan in 1945, when we were a country of 48 states.

They were playing in Wrigley Field on October 14, 2003, up three games to two against Florida and leading 3–0 in the eighth inning of Game 6 of the National League Championship Series, when the Marlins' Luis Castillo lifted a fly ball toward the left-field stands.

Moises Alou, who'd been influential in the Marlins' improbable World Series victory in 1997, drifted over to the wall in foul territory and jumped, reaching his glove into the seats.

That's when the baseball world met a fan named Steve Bartman.

Wearing headphones over his Cubs cap, Bartman got up out of his chair and interfered with Alou's attempt to catch the ball.

Bartman was not alone, only the most prominent. The ball bounced off of him and into the stands. The Cubs were denied a ruling of fan interference because the ball had left the field of play.

Instead of recording the second out of the eighth inning, Castillo got a new life, eventually walking to put runners at first and second. At light speed, it took Florida just eight pitches to tie the game 3–3. In a pivotal sequence, shortstop Alex Gonzalez muffed a potential inning-ending double-play grounder that extended the Marlins' rally.

Alex Gonzalez led all National League shortstops in fielding percentage that season.

With eight runs and five hits later collected in that fateful eighth inning, thanks in part to the Cubs and their fans, Florida had tied the NLCS at three games apiece.

If it is possible, the Cubs made it even more excruciating for their fans in Game 7. They built Kerry Wood a 5–3 lead only to lose 9–6.

The Marlins continued their march of upsets, beating the New York Yankees in six games to win their second World Series since 1997.

The 2003 National League Championship Series is remembered forever in Chicago for the ball that wasn't caught.

The Cubs, who have had uncommon good luck in years ending in '08, the year of their last world championship, were considered the best team in the National League in 2008.

The luck wasn't *that* good.

His Final Act as a Yankee (2003)

Speaking of futility, the Red Sox hadn't won a World Series since Babe Ruth was in their clubhouse, presumably drinking their beer, in 1918.

In the 2003 American League Championship Series, they trailed the archrival Yankees three games to two heading back to New York. The Sox then came from behind to win Game 6, 9–6.

They were protecting a 5–2 lead in the eighth inning of Game 7 when manager Grady Little inexplicably left a tiring Pedro Martinez on the mound. That decision was instrumental in eventually costing him his job.

A three-run Yankees rally tied the game.

It should be noted that there would have been no opportunity for a Yankees comeback were it not for Mike Mussina. Pitching in relief for the first time in his career, he tossed three innings of two-hit shutout ball, striking out three.

Enter Aaron Boone, literally.

Boone, a National League all-star that season with Cincinnati and acquired by the Yankees soon thereafter, was inserted into the game as a pinch runner during the uprising and took over third base in the ninth inning.

With the teams tied at 5–5 in the 11th inning, and with the winner going to the World Series, Boone approached the plate for his first at bat of the game, against knuckleballer Tim Wakefield—who had pitched a scoreless 10th inning—with the idea of swinging at the first pitch from a pitcher against whom he had not had much prior success.

That first pitch was a do-nothing knuckleball.

Boone swung.

The result was a fly ball that landed in the left-field stands, etched his name in Yankees lore, and sent Yankee Stadium into one of the classic postseason moments of frenzy.

The frenzy ended for the Yankees when they lost the World Series to Florida in six games.

In a cruel irony, it turned out to be the end of Aaron Boone's short career with the team. On January 16, 2004, in what he would call a freak accident, Boone tore the anterior cruciate ligament in his left knee while playing a pickup basketball game, an activity expressly banned in his Yankees contract.

The ball club voided his contract, an event that led directly to the acquisition of his replacement, Alex Rodriguez.

The Curse, Reversed (2004)

It seemed like more of the same for the Red Sox the following year.

The Yankees beat the Red Sox at Fenway Park in the third game of the American League Championship Series, 19–8, to take a three-games-to-none lead.

If any Red Sox fans had gone to Logan Airport to board a flight to Las Vegas with the express intent of putting money on the Sox to win the next four games, no casino would have taken their bet. It would have been off the board.

Who could imagine that this would be the last Yankees win of the season, especially given the historical context? No team in history had ever rallied from a three-game deficit to win a seven-game series.

Ever.

The Yankees led 4–3 at Fenway in Game 4 and called on Mariano Rivera in the eighth inning for a two-inning save.

In the ninth, Rivera walked Kevin Millar. Dave Roberts, a speedy outfielder acquired during the season by Boston on the trading deadline from the Los Angeles Dodgers, was inserted to pinch-run for Millar.

The only people who may not have known that Roberts was in the game to steal second and put the potential tying run into scoring position were in the adjoining galaxy. Rivera, acutely aware of the threat, threw over to first base three times to keep Roberts close.

On the first pitch to Bill Mueller, Roberts broke for second.

Jorge Posada's strong throw was over the second-base bag but to the shortstop side. Roberts was safe and in scoring position.

 With Rivera's impeccable control, why didn't Joe Torre have him pitch out repeatedly, since Roberts's intentions were obvious?

Mueller promptly singled to center, scoring Roberts to tie the game.

After the two teams had traded scoring opportunities in the 11th inning, Manny Ramirez led off the bottom of the 12th with a single against reliever Paul Quantrill, who was beginning his first inning of work. David Ortiz followed with a home run to right field.

Boston 6, New York 4.

 David Ortiz became the first player ever to hit two walk-off homers in the same postseason, his first one having ended the Divisional Series against the Anaheim Angels.

Ortiz also won Game 5, with a run-scoring single in the 14th inning, sending the series back to New York for the Legend of the Bloody Sock in Game 6 (in which Boston pitcher Curt Schilling's ankle had spotted blood on his sock, as a result of the fresh stitches that were keeping him in the game) and a lopsided Boston victory in Game 7.

The Red Sox danced on the field at Yankee Stadium and never lost again in 2004, sweeping the St. Louis Cardinals for their first World Series victory since 1918.

 For generations, the Red Sox lived and died with the long ball. Power was their game. How ironic that a stolen base was pivotal in one of the greatest wins in franchise history.

A Tiger by the Tail (2006)

Putting money on the Red Sox to win games four through seven against the Yankees in the 2004 American League Championship would not be the only bet Las Vegas would not in good conscience take.

How about trying to plunk money down on the Detroit Tigers' making it to the 2006 World Series after a dozen consecutive losing seasons?

Now, really.

They were just three years removed from a 119-loss season. In 2005, they lost 91 games in a season best remembered for Alan Trammell's firing as manager. And in April, starting off the season with a 7–7 record, there was no reason to believe it would be anything but more of the same.

After a particularly dispiriting loss, manager Jim Leyland, having decided he had seen enough lackadaisical effort, called a meeting wherein he proceeded to air out his team. All Leyland asked from his players was for them to play hard for nine innings. From there, the Tigers took off, winning 28 of their next 35 games. Eventually, they were 40 games over .500 and finished with 95 victories.

On the negative side, over the last third of the season, they lost 31 of their final 50 games, including the final five in a row, which cost them the American League Central Division title. Nonetheless, they made the play-offs as the wild-card team.

After losing the opening game of the Division Series against the Yankees in New York, they won the next three to advance to the American League Championship Series against Oakland.

The Tigers were intent on a four-game sweep but were trailing the Athletics 3–0 in Game 4.

That's when Magglio Ordonez went to work. Ordonez had been signed at age 17 in Venezuela by the White Sox. They considered him an average prospect. He spent more than six years in the minor leagues, the first five at Class-A or lower. He batted approximately three thousand times as a pro before reaching the majors. Eventually, he grew into a four-time American League all-star before signing with the Tigers as a free agent. As recipient of a five-year, $75 million contract, he came to represent the eager desperation of a lost franchise. But here in Game 4 of the ALCS, Magglio Ordonez homered to tie the game in the sixth inning.

Up again in the ninth inning with two outs and the score still tied 3–3, Ordonez, facing Oakland closer Huston Street, hit a three-run homer into the left-field seats to send Detroit to its first World Series in 22 years.

It marked the eighth time in history that a postseason series had ended with a home run.

A subsequent 4–1 World Series loss to St. Louis did not diminish the Tigers' remarkable turnaround.

Beyond the Box Score

It would take the Tigers another three seasons to knock on the postseason's door again, but in 2009 they were poised to win their division for the first time since 1987 (a distinction they would have earned in 2006 had they not gotten swept at home in the final series of the season against last-place Kansas City, relegating them to wild-card status). Detroit had secured sole possession of first place in May and stood confident on top of the standings with a seven-game lead over the Twins on September 6. It all came crashing down as Minnesota came storming back to tie them for the division title on the last day of the season—winning a one-game playoff in extra innings to advance to the Divisional Series. Never before had a team three games behind with four left made the postseason.

2007: A Season of Momentous Milestones

No milestone was bigger in 2007 than Atlanta manager Bobby Cox being ejected from game 132 of his Hall of Fame career on August 14. Ironically, he was asked to—as they said in *The Odd Couple*—"remove himself from the premises" against the San Francisco Giants. The old record was held for generations by John McGraw, who led the Giants' forebears in New York.

The year 2007 also saw Trevor Hoffman, who started out in the Cincinnati system as a shortstop and resorted to pitching as a last resort, become the first relief pitcher ever to record 500 saves. He accomplished the feat on June 6, at home in San Diego against the rival Los Angeles Dodgers.

Trevor Hoffman may have the most saves of any reliever in baseball history, but the biggest save of his life was made by a pediatrician who, when Hoffman was six weeks old, discovered and removed a damaged right kidney that had a blockage. Going through life with one healthy kidney, he had to sign a medical waiver to play at the University of Arizona.

This was also the first season in history whereby three players struck their 500th career home run. The first was Toronto designated hitter Frank Thomas. On June 28, he circled the bases in the Metrodome in the Twin Cities, ironically the ballpark in which he struck his first major-league home run.

Next up was the Yankees' Alex Rodriguez. On August 4, at Yankee Stadium, he hit number 500 against Kansas City. At thirty-two years and eight days, he gained the distinction of becoming the youngest player to do so.

Then, on September 16, against the Los Angeles Angels, Jim Thome of the White Sox did something in Chicago with his 500th that no one had done before: deliver a walk-off home run in a win against the Los Angeles Angels.

Also that season on June 20, Sammy Sosa, back with the Texas Rangers, the team of his major-league birth, struck his 600th against, ironically, the Chicago Cubs, the team with whom he gained fame. He was the fifth hitter in history to do so.

Oh, yeah, I almost forgot. . .

On August 7, Barry Bonds became baseball's all-time home run king—though that claim remains highly dubious in the minds of many—when he surpassed the great Hank Aaron with home run number 756 against Washington's Mike Bacsik. Less than two months later, the Giants couldn't wait to cut ties with Bonds after 15 seasons. He and his 762 homers never played again.

Finally, remember in math class in high school when the teacher would pose a question that began with "Two trains traveling in opposite directions . . ."?

In perhaps the greatest collapse in major-league history, the New York Mets squandered a 7-game lead with just 17 to play, handing the Eastern Division title in the National League to the Philadelphia Phillies on the final day of the season. It would be the first of three consecutive NL East titles for Philly, helping the franchise redeem its own collapse of 1964, in which they squandered a 6½-game lead over the final week of the season.

The Mets stuck the knife in that season and, astonishingly, managed to twist it further the following year, losing a potential playoff bid *again* on the final day of the season. Both times the Amazin's amazingly dropped game 162 to the Florida Marlins.

Fortunately for Mets fans, there was no worry over having their hopes raised and then dashed at the end of the 2009 season. The team took an unusual route to avoiding a September collapse by scheduling it for June instead, as an all-star lineup of injuries paved the way for more than 90 losses and a fourth-place finish.

Meanwhile, whizzing by in the opposite direction, the Colorado Rockies won 11 straight games in September and 14 of 15 to propel them to the playoffs for the first time in a dozen years and their first World Series in franchise history, which they lost to Boston.

It was the Red Sox' second title in four Series.

Yawn.

The Rockies would return to the playoffs in 2009 as the NL wild card after starting the season at 18–28 and firing manager Clint Hurdle.

The Devil Is in the Details (2008)

For years, the Tampa–St. Pete area was collateral—collateral as threat to relocate major-league franchises seeking new stadiums in their hometowns.

Over the years, the San Francisco Giants, Minnesota Twins, Seattle Mariners, and Chicago White Sox used Tampa–St. Pete as a bargaining chip, threatening to pack the trunks if they did not receive a new playpen.

In 1992, the Giants were sold to a local Tampa group and were gone until the National League stepped in and found Bob Lurie, a local buyer, to save the franchise by the Bay (not Tampa Bay).

In Chicago's case, team owner Jerry Reinsdorf kept the Illinois state legislature in session all night to get his way.

Finally, in 1995, Tampa was granted an expansion franchise in the American League that would begin play three years later.

Right out of the womb, there were problems.

At the expansion draft held in Phoenix on November 18, 1997, the so-called Devil Rays drafted an outfielder, unprotected by the Houston Astros, named Bobby Abreu. Moments later, they decided they just had to have Kevin Stocker to play shortstop and traded Abreu to Philadelphia.

Stocker gave Tampa Bay nothing.

Abreu gave Philadelphia four 100-RBI seasons and collected seven straight through 2009.

Playing in the toughest division in baseball, the American League East, the Rays finished in last place every year except 2004. In November 2007, the Rays decided that changing their name might induce a change of luck.

Gone was the "Devil," and they resurfaced as the Tampa Bay Rays.

The rechristening worked.

The Rays, under the direction of erudite manager Joe Maddon, not only experienced their first winning season, they finished in first place. In the playoffs, they dispatched the Chicago White Sox with ease before standing up to the defending champion Boston Red Sox, winning the seventh game of the American League Championship Series and advancing to their first World Series before losing to the Philadelphia Phillies.

Tampa Bay didn't shine as bright in 2009, but the Rays still managed to finish above .500 for only the second time in franchise history. It was only enough for third place in the AL East, as the Rays were behind both the wild-card Red Sox and a resurgent Yankee team that christened their new stadium by taking home its 27th World Series title.

Twenty-Five Meanderings, Minutiae, and Miscellaneous Fun Facts

1. Rusty Staub is the only player ever with 500 or more hits with four different teams.

2. Fernando Tatis, playing for St. Louis in 1999, remains the only player ever to hit two grand slams in the same inning. And he hit them off the same pitcher, Chan Ho Park, of the Dodgers, in Los Angeles.

3. Tony Cloninger, playing for the Atlanta Braves, is the only pitcher to hit two grand slams in the same game, which he did July 3, 1966.

4. The New York Yankees lost the 1960 World Series despite batting a collective .338.

5. The Pittsburgh Pirates won the 1960 World Series with a team earned run average of 7.11.

6. Rennie Stennett, of the Pittsburgh Pirates, is the only player to get seven hits in a nine-inning game.

7. Rod Carew, of the Minnesota Twins, won the 1972 American League batting title without having hit a home run.

8. Al Benton, of the 1934 Philadelphia Athletics and 1952 Boston Red Sox, is the only pitcher to have faced Babe Ruth and Mickey Mantle.

9. The same guy pinch-hit for Ted Williams and Carl Yastrzemski: Carroll Hardy.

10. Stan Musial gathered 3,630 career hits, 1,815 in St. Louis, 1,815 on the road.

11. Warren Spahn won 363 games and had 363 career hits.

12. Fred Lynn, of Boston, in 1975 and Ichiro Suzuki, of the 2001 Seattle Mariners, are the only two players to win the Rookie of the Year Award and Most Valuable Player Award in the same season.

13. Fernando Valenzuela, of the 1981 Los Angeles Dodgers, is the only pitcher to win the Rookie of the Year Award and Cy Young Award in the same season.

14. Frank Robinson won the National League Most Valuable Player Award in Cincinnati in 1961 and the American League Most Valuable Player Award in Baltimore in 1966, the only player to win in each league.

15. Frank Robinson is the only player to win the Rookie of the Year Award, the Most Valuable Player Award, and the Triple Crown.

16. Ralph Kiner, of the Pittsburgh Pirates, led the National League a record seven consecutive seasons in home runs.

17. Cesar Geronimo was the 3,000th career strikeout victim of both Bob Gibson and Nolan Ryan.

18. Rookie Willie Mays was on deck when Bobby Thomson hit the "Shot Heard Round the World" off of Ralph Branca, October 3, 1951.

19. Hall of Famer Dave Winfield was born October 3, 1951.

20. Hall of Famer Brooks Robinson hit into four triple plays in his career.

21. Joe DiMaggio hit 361 home runs but struck out only 369 times in his career.

22. Catcher Harry Chiti is the only player ever traded for himself, from Cleveland to the New York Mets for a player to be named later: Harry Chiti.

23. Hall of Fame pitcher Hoyt Wilhelm did not win his first game until age 29.

24. Bill Voiselle is the only player to wear his hometown on his back, number 96, in honor of Ninety Six, South Carolina.

25. Babe Ruth ended the 1926 World Series when he was out attempting to steal second base.

Index

Aaron, Henry Louis (Hank), 37, 64, 122, 125–27, 170, 182, 199, 200, 218
Abbott, Jim, 10
Abbreviations, for stats, 132
Abreu, Bobby, 220
Aerobic exercises, for pitchers, 70
African-American players, 29
Aguilera, Rick, 95
Alexander, Grover Cleveland, 30
All-Star Game, 119, 191
Alomar, Roberto, 78, 129
Alou, Matty, 37
Alou, Moises, 23, 37, 205, 210
Alston, Walter, 100
Altitude, baseball distance and, 74
Amaro, Ruben, Jr., 145
American Association, 29, 188
American League (AL), 54, 84, 118–19, 185, 188–89
    designated hitters and, 121–22
Aparicio, Luis, 129
Appling, Luke, 35
Arizona Diamondbacks, 206–9
Armas, Tony, 168
Atlanta Braves, 83
Autry, Gene, 168

Babe Ruth era, of baseball, 30–31
Backman, Wally, 170
Bacsik, Mike, 218
Baines, Harold, 122
Baker, Del, 36
Baker, Dusty, 78

Balance Point drill, 70
Balaz, John, 77
Balk, defined, 17
Ball, defined, 17
Ball trajectory, hitting and, 47
Baltimore Orioles, 54
Banks, Ernie, 64
Barfield, Jesse, 167
Barometric pressure, baseball distance and, 75
Barrett, Marty, 170
Bartman, Steve, 23, 210
Base coaches, defined, 17
Base on balls, defined, 18
Baseball
    Babe Ruth era of, 30–33
    basic rules of, 13–15
    dawn and rise of free agency in, 151–83
    dead ball era of, 29–30
    divisional play (1968–1975), 117–28
    early history of, 27–29
    eternity of, 8–11
    evening games and, 120–21
    expansion era of, 83–96
    fantasy, 146–50
    field, 15–16
    fun facts about, 221–23
    future of, 8–9
    golden age of, 53–63
    hope and, 3–8
    language of, 17–26
    love of, 1–3
    wild-card era of, 193–223

Baseball diamond, 15–16
Baseball gear, holy trinity of, 71
Baseballs, 71. *See also* Curveballs; Fastballs; Hitting;
    Pitching
    altitude factors affecting distance of, 74
    barometric pressure factors affecting distance
        of, 75
    curves, 73–74
    dynamics of, 72
    humidity factors affecting distance of, 75
    interaction with bats and, 71–72
    temperature factors affecting distance of, 75
    wind factors affecting distance of, 75
Bats, 49–51, 71. *See also* Hitting; Hitters
    interaction with baseballs and, 71–72
Battery, defined, 18
Batting. *See* Hitting
Batting average (BA), 133
Baylor, Don, 168
Beane, Billy, 145–46
Belanger, Mark, 129
Belinda, Stan, 180, 181
Belle, Albert, 10
Bench, Johnny, 129
Benitez, Armando, 201, 203
Benton, Al, 222
Berra, Yogi, 10, 61, 88, 167, 186
Berryhill, Damon, 179
Billingham, Jack, 126
Billy Ball, 98
Billy Burnout, 98
Blyleven, Bert, 81
Boggs, Wade, 37, 175
Bonds, Barry, 51, 127, 180, 205, 218
Boone, Aaron, 211–12
Boone, Bob, 158
Borgmann, Glenn, 77
Boston Braves, 83
Boston Red Sox, 127, 145, 211–14, 219
Boudreau, Lou, 107
Bourn, Michael, 111, 115
Bowa, Larry, 129
Boyer, Clete, 129
Branca, Ralph, 57, 60, 222
Braun, Ryan, 150
Bream, Sid, 179–81
Brett, George, 37, 41–42, 159–61
Brinkman, Joe, 159
Brock, Lou, 177
Brodeur, Martin, 6
Brooklyn Dodgers, 53, 54, 59, 61
Brosius, Scott, 207
Brown, Gates, 76
Bryant, Kobe, 6
Buck, Jack, 163

Buckner, Bill, 169–70, 173
Budig, Gene, 203
Bunts
    defined, 18
    sacrifice, 106
Burroughs, Jeff, 155
Bush, George W., 207

Cabrera, Francisco, 179, 180
California Angels, 167–69
Carew, Rod, 221
Carlton, Steve, 80, 174
Carter, Gary, 170
Carter, Joe, 44, 181–83
Cartwright, Alexander, 28
Carty, Rico, 122
Cash, Norm, 76
Castillo, Luis, 23, 114, 210
Catcher's box, defined, 18
Catcher's interference, defined, 18
Cater, Danny, 117
Cepeda, Orlando, 122
Chamblis, Chris, 124, 152–53
Changeup pitch, 66
Chicago Cubs, 209–11
Chiti, Harry, 223
Cincinnati Red Stockings, 28
Clark, Al, 157
Clark, Jack, 164, 165
Clark, Will, 37
Clemens, Roger, 80, 81, 207
Clemente, Roberto, 37, 129
Cleveland Indians, 60, 65
Cloninger, Tony, 221
Cobb, Ty, 114, 162, 199
Coleman, Vince, 114
Colorado Rockies, 119, 219
Continental League, 84–86
Cooperstown, New York, 27
Cora, Joey, 200
Corcoran, Larry, 77
Corrales, Pat, 99
Counsell, Craig, 204
Countdown to contact, for hitting, 45
Cox, Bobby, 97, 217
Crawford, Carl, 110, 115
Cronin, Joe, 35
Crosetti, Frank, 62
Culberson, Leon, 55
Curveballs, 73–74

Darcy, Pat, 128
Davis, Mike, 172
Davis, Tommy, 77, 122
Dawson, Andre, 129

Dead ball, defined, 18
Defensive interference, 22
Defensive replacements, 103–4
Delivery, for fastballs, 67
Denkinger, Don, 165–66
Dent, Bucky, 155–57
Designated hitters, 13, 121–23
Detroit Tigers, 215–16
Diamond, baseball, 15–16
Dickey, Bill, 35, 37
DiMaggio, Joe, 35, 36, 50, 53, 54, 55, 59, 90, 169, 198, 223
Dineen, Bill, 188
Divisional play, history of, 189–90
Doerr, Bobby, 35
Dombrowski, Dave, 204
Double play, defined, 19
Double switch, 102
Doubleday, Abner, 188
Doubleheader, defined, 18
Downing, Al, 126, 200
Downing, Brian, 168
Dressen, Chuck, 60
Drysdale, Don, 94

Earned run average (ERA), 134
Easler, Mike, 42
Eckersley, Dennis, 95, 172
Edmonds, Jim, 129
Eisenhower, Dwight D., 207
Elbow, elevating, for fastballs, 68
Ellsbury, Jacoby, 111, 115
Equipment, baseball, holy trinity of, 71
Espinosa, Alvaro, 177
Evans, Jim, 76
Evening games, 120–21
Expansion era, of baseball, 83–96

Face, Elroy, 96
Fair ball, defined, 19
Fair territory, defined, 19
Fan (spectator) interference, 23
Fantasy baseball, 146–47
    drafting teams for, 147–50
Fastballs. *See also* Baseballs; Pitching
    delivery for, 67
    elevating elbow for, 68
    follow-through for, 68–69
    grip for, 66
    hand on top for, 68
    mechanics of, 66–69
    starting position for, 66–67
    stretch for, 68
Feller, Bob, 35, 53, 77, 79
Fernandez, Tony, 201

Field, baseball, 15–16
Fielders, greatest, 129
Fielder's choice, defined, 19–20
Figgins, Chone, 115
Fingers, Rollie, 95
Finley, Charlie, 23, 120
Finley, Steve, 206
First-base coach, 17
Fisher, Jack, 91, 92
Fisk, Carlton, 127–28
Florida Marlins, 119, 204–5, 210–11, 219
Follow-through, for fastballs, 68–69
Force play, defined, 20
Ford, Whitey, 81
Fosse, Ray, 119
Foul ball, defined, 19, 20–21
Foul tip, defined, 21
Four-seam grip, 66
Fowler, Dexter, 110
Fox, Nellie, 129
Foxx, Jimmie, 35, 64, 182
Franco, John, 95
Frazee, Harry, 30–31
Free agency, dawn and rise of, 151–83
Fregosi, Jim, 79, 181
Frey, Jim, 98
Frick, Ford, 90, 91
Fun facts, about baseball, 221–23

Gamson, William, 147
Gant, Ron, 178
Garciaparra, Nomar, 37
Garr, Ralph, 37
Gear, baseball, holy trinity of, 71
Gehrig, Lou, 32, 33–35, 182, 199
Geronimo, Cesar, 222
Giamatti, A. Bartlett, 6–7
Giambi, Jason, 107
Giambi, Jeremy, 205, 206
Gibson, Bob, 80, 81, 117, 222
Gibson, Kirk, 171–73
Giles, Warren, 85
Gilliam, Jim, 109
Gillick, Pat, 145
Gionfriddo, Al, 58–59
Glavine, Tom, 80
Golden age, of baseball, 53–63
Gonzalez, Alex, 210
Gonzalez, Luis, 208–9
Gordon, Joe, 35
Goryl, Johnny, 32
Gossage, Goose, 96
Grabarkewitz, Billy, 119
Grace, Mark, 37
Grebey, Ray, 197

Greenberg, Hank, 37, 53
Grich, Bobby, 129, 168
Griffey, Ken, Jr., 64, 129, 200–201
Grip, pitcher's, 66
    four-seam, 66
    two-seam, 66
Grip Strengthening drill, 70
Guerrero, Vladimir, 37, 129
Guidry, Ron, 160
Gwynn, Tony, 37, 197

Hall, Donald, 6
Halladay, Roy, 6, 81, 150
Hammaker, Atlee, 159
Hand on top, for fastballs, 68
Hanrahan, Joel, 15
Hartnett, Charles Leo "Gabby," 33
Hatten, Joe, 59
Helton, Todd, 37
Henderson, Dave, 168–69, 170, 177
Henderson, Rickey, 98, 114, 175–77
Henderson, Steve, 41
Henke, Tom, 96
Herman, Billy, 35
Hermanski, Gene, 59
Hernandez, Keith, 129, 170
Hernandez, Roberto, 95
Herzog, Whitey, 98, 158, 165
Heydler, John, 121
Hickman, Jim, 119
Hillerich, John "Bud," 49
Hillerich & Bradsby Co., 49
Hit-and-run, 103
Hitters
    building lineup of, 108–9
    greatest, 37
    greatest, for 500 Home Run Club, 51
    statistics for, 132–34
    what they look for in pitches, 47
Hitting. *See also* Bats
    art of, 39–40
    ball trajectory and, 47
    countdown to contact and, 45
    guessing and, 47
    physics of, 48–51
    soft-centered focus and, 44
    swinging and, 45–46
    theories of, 40–43
    vision and, 43–44
Hobs, Roy, 171
Hoffman, Trevor, 95, 217
Holds (H), 134
Holy trinity, of baseball gear, 71
Home base, stealing, 113–14
Home plate, shape and dimensions of, 16

Home Run Club, 51
Hope, baseball and, 3–8
Hopkins, Gail, 76
Hornsby, Rogers, 50
Hough, Charlie, 154
Houk, Ralph, 123
Howard, Ryan, 107
Hriniak, Walt, 42
Hubbell, Carl, 35, 167
Huizenga, Wayne, 204
Humidity, baseball distance and, 75
Hunter, Catfish, 81
Hunter, Torii, 129, 150

Illegal pitch, defined, 21
Infield, bringing in, 104–5
Infield fly, defined, 21–22
Innings, number of, 14–15
Innings pitched (IP), 135
Intentional walks, 101
Interference
    defensive, 22
    defined, 22–23
    offensive, 22
    spectator (fan), 23
    umpire's, 22–23
Iorg, Dane, 165

Jackson, Reggie, 64, 122, 153–54, 182
Jackson, Shoeless Joe, 31
Jackson, Vincent Edward "Bo," 174–75
James, Bill, 144–45
James, LeBron, 6
Jenkins, Ferguson, 81
Jeter, Derek, 8, 37, 201, 202, 206, 207
John, Tommy, 81
Johnson, Charles, 129
Johnson, Davey, 203
Johnson, Randy, 30, 80, 200, 206–7, 208–9
Johnson, Walter, 30
Jones, Andruw, 129
Jones, Chipper, 37
Jones, Doug, 96
Jones, Ruppert, 169
Jones, Todd, 95
Justice, Dave, 179

Kaat, Jim, 81
Kaline, Al, 129
Keeler, Willie, 39
Kekich, Mike, 123–24
Kellert, Bill, 61
Keltner, Ken, 36
Killebrew, Harmon, 64
Kim, Byung-Hyun, 207

Kiner, Ralph, 222
Knight, Ray, 170, 171
Knoblauch, Chuck, 207
Koenig, Mark, 32
Koosman, Jerry, 79
Koufax, Sandy, 77, 80, 81, 92–95
Kuhn, Bowie, 124, 126

Landex, Stan, 89
Language, of baseball, 17–26
Larsen, Don, 10, 61–62, 89
LaRussa, Tony, 97
Lasorda, Tommy, 164
Lavalliere, Mike, 180
Leadoff hitters, 108
Leary, Tim, 177
Lee, Manny, 78
Left-handed batters, 107
Leibrandt, Charlie, 178
Lewis, Michael, 146
Leyland, Jim, 97, 215
Lineups, building, 108–9
Linz, Phil, 93
Littell, Mark, 152
Little, Grady, 211
Lockouts, in Major League Baseball, 194–98
Long Toss drill, 69
Lopez, Al, 35
Los Angeles Angels, 86
Los Angeles Dodgers, 65
Losses (L), 135–36
Louisville Slugger, 49
Luciano, Ron, 76
Lyle, Sparky, 96
Lynn, Fred, 128, 158, 159, 222

Mack, Connie, 121
MacPhail, Lee, 161
Maddon, Joe, 220
Maddox, Gary, 129
Maddux, Greg, 80, 118
Madlock, Bill, 37, 179
Maier, Jeffrey, 201–4
Major League Baseball (MLB), 83, 84, 185
    lockouts and strikes in history of, 194–98
Maloney, Jim, 77
Managerial strategies, 97–98
Managers
    decisions and, 101–14
    functions of, 99–101
    importance of, 98–99
Manning, Eli, 6
Mantle, Mickey, 54, 64, 90–91, 222
Marichal, Juan, 81
Maris, Roger, 14, 90–92, 129

Marsh, Randy, 181
Martin, Billy, 98–99, 107, 159, 160
Martinez, Edgar, 37, 122, 200
Martinez, Pedro, 81, 211
Martinez, Tino, 207
Mason, Roger, 181
Mathews, Eddie, 64, 182
Mathewson, Christy, 30
Mattingly, Don, 37, 129, 161, 167
Mauch, Gene, 100, 167
Mauer, Joe, 150
Mays, Willie, 37, 54, 60, 64, 126, 129, 175, 182, 198, 222
Mazeroski, William Stanley (Bill), 4, 88–89, 129, 168, 183
McCarthy, Joe, 32
McClelland, Tim, 159–60
McCovey, Willie, 43–44, 64, 107
McGraw, Tug, 158
McGwire, Mark, 51, 205
McKeon, Jack, 76
McLain, Denny, 117
McNally, Dave, 151
McRae, Brian, 42
McRae, Hal, 122, 161–62
McSherry, John, 181
Medwick, Joe, 35
Mendoza, Mario, 102
Meoli, Rudy, 76
Mesa, Jose, 95, 204
Messersmith, Andy, 151
Mickey, Willie, 54
Miksis, Eddie, 59
Millar, Kevin, 213
Miller, Marvin, 197
Milwaukee Braves, 83
Milwaukee Brewers, 167
Minnesota Twins, 84
Mitchell, Dale, 37, 63
Mitchell, Kevin, 170–71, 173–74
Mize, Johnny, 35, 37
Molina, Yadier, 129
Molitor, Paul, 37, 41, 122
Moneyball (Lewis), 146
Montgomery, Jeff, 96
Montreal Expos, 84, 86
Moore, Donnie, 168
Morris, Jack, 81
Mueller, Bill, 213–14
Munson, Thurman, 160
Murphy, Dwayne, 129
Murray, Eddie, 64
Murray, Jim, 176
Murtaugh, Danny, 120
Musial, Stan, 37, 53, 126, 222

Mussina, Mike, 205, 211
Myers, Randy, 95

Nagy, Charles, 204
National Association of Base Ball Players, 28
National Association of Professional Baseball
    Leagues, 29, 188
National League (NL), 29, 83, 118–19, 185, 188–89
    designated hitters and, 121–22
National League of Professional Base Ball Clubs, 28
Nen, Robb, 95
Nettles, Graig, 129, 160
New York Giants, 59, 60
New York Knickerbockers, 28
New York Mets, 118, 218–19, 219
New York Yankees, 4, 53, 59, 61, 62, 206–8, 211–14,
    221
    Babe Ruth traded to, 30–31
    Casey Stengel and, 54
    wildest trade of, 123–24
Newcombe, Don, 60
Niedenfuer, Tom, 163, 164
Niekro, Phil, 80
Night games, 120–21
Nokes, Matt, 177
Number eight hitters, 109
Number five hitters, 109
Number four hitters, 109
Number nine hitters, 109
Number seven hitters, 109
Number six hitters, 109
Number three hitters, 108
Number two hitters, 108

Oakland Athletics, 65, 83, 98
Obstruction, defined, 23
Offensive interference, 22
Official at bats (AB), 132
Okrent, Daniel, 146
Oliva, Tony, 37, 122
Oliver, Al, 37
On-base percentage (OBP), 133
Ordonez, Magglio, 37, 215–16
Ortiz, David, 107, 214
Otis, Amos, 119
Ott, Mel, 35, 64
Overslide, defined, 24
Ovetchkin, Alex, 6

Palm ball, 66
Palmeiro, Rafael, 51
Palmer, Jim, 81
Park, Chan Ho, 221
Parker, David, 129
Parker, Wes, 129

Passeau, Claude, 35
Pena, Carlos, 41
Pena, Tony, 129
Percival, Troy, 95
Perry, Gaylord, 80, 160
Peskey, Johnny, 55, 128
Peterson, Fritz, 123–24
Pettis, Gary, 78, 129
Philadelphia Phillies, 157–58
Phillips, Dave, 161
Phillips, Richie, 202, 203
Piazza, Mike, 37
Pickups, 70
Pierre, Juan, 114
Pinson, Vada, 129
Pipp, Wally, 35
Pitchers
    greatest relief, 95–96
    greatest starting, 80–81
    legislation against, 118
    statistics for, 134–36
Pitching. *See also* Baseballs, Fastballs
    art of, 65
    curveballs, 73–74
    mechanics of, 66–69
    recommended drills for, 69–70
    working on one component at a time for, 69
Pitching trajectories, 72
Pittsburg Pirates, 4, 221
Plate appearance (PA), 133
Podsednik, Scott, 114
Posada, Jorge, 205, 206, 207, 213
Position numbers, 136
Power, Vic, 129
Puckett, Kirby, 37, 177–78
Puhl, Terry, 77
Pujols, Albert, 6, 37, 150

Quality starts (QS), 135
Quantrill, Paul, 214

Raines, Tim, 114
Ramirez, Manny, 37, 51, 150, 214
Randolph, Willie, 78
Reardon, Jeff, 95
Reinsdorf, Jerry, 220
Reitz, Ken, 129
Remy, Jerry, 77
Renteria, Edgar, 204
Reserve system, 151
Reuschel, Rick, 175
Reyes, Jose, 114
Reynolds, Allie, 76–77
Richardson, Bobby, 43
Rickey, Branch, 57, 58, 85

Right-handed batters, 107
Rigney, Bill, 60
Ripken, Cal, Jr., 167, 198–99
Rivera, Mariano, 8, 95, 140, 203, 208, 213
Rivers, Mickey, 156
Rizzuto, Phil, 36, 176
Roberts, Dave, 213
Roberts, Robin, 81
Robinson, Brooks, 129, 223
Robinson, Frank, 182, 222
Robinson, Jackie, 37, 53, 55–58, 61, 85, 122, 198
Robinson, Rachel, 61
Rodriguez, Alex, 37, 51, 150, 152, 212, 217–18
Rodriguez, Aurelio, 129
Rodriguez, Ivan, 129
Rolen, Scott, 129
Rollins, Jimmy, 114
Roosevelt, Franklin D., 33
Root, Charlie, 31
Rose, Pete, 37, 119, 158, 162–63, 176, 199
Roseboro, Johnny, 94
Rotisserie League Baseball, 146
Rudi, Joe, 129
Ruffing, Red, 35
Rules, basic, of baseball, 13–15
Rundown, defined, 24
Runs (R), 133
Runs batted in (RBIs), 133
Ruth, George Herman "Babe," 30–33, 50, 64, 90–91, 122, 154, 170, 182, 199, 222, 223
    called shot of, 31–33
    traded Yankees, 30–31
Ryan, Nolan, 76–80, 222
Ryan, Sandy, 78

Sabathia, C. C., 8, 152
Sabermetrics, 144–46
Sacrifice bunts, 106
Safety squeeze, 24
Sain, Johnny, 57
Sanguillen, Manny, 129
Santiago, Benito, 129
Saves (S), 135
Schilling, Curt, 206–7, 214
Schmidt, Mike, 64, 182
Scioscia, Mike, 77
Scorecards, 136–44. *See also* Stats (statistics)
Scores, keeping, 136–44
Scott, George, 129
Scully, Vin, 170
Seattle Mariners, 118, 145
Seattle Pilots, 118
Seaver, Tom, 79, 80
Second base, stealing, 112–13
Seitz, Peter, 151–52

Selig, Bud, 190, 193–94
Set position, defined, 24
Shea, Bill, 84–85
Sheffield, Gary, 51
Sherry, Norm, 93
Shifts, strategy of, 106–7
Shotton, Burt, 59
Signals, manager, 109–10
Sit-ups, 69
Slaughter, Enos, 35, 55
Slip pitch, 66
Slugging percentage (SLG), 134
Small ball, 30
Smith, Lee, 95
Smith, Ozzie, 129, 155, 163–64, 173
Smith, Red, 3
Smoltz, John, 81
Snider, Duke, 54
Snow, Eric, 162
Snow, J. T., 129
Soft-centered focus, hitting and, 45
Soriano, Alfonso, 115, 207, 208
Sosa, Elias, 154
Sosa, Sammy, 51, 205, 218
Sotomayor, Sonya, 197–98
Spahn, Warren, 80, 99, 222
Speaker, Tris, 31
Spectator (fan) interference, 23
Spencer, Shane, 205
Squeeze play, defined, 24
St. Louis Cardinals, 65, 83
Stallard, Tracy, 91, 92
Standings, determining, 185–88
Stanley, Bob, 171
Stargell, Willie, 182
Starting position, for fastballs, 66–67
Stats (statistics). *See also* Scorecards
    abbreviations for, 132
    for hitters, 132–34
    for pitchers, 134–36
Staub, Rusty, 221
Stealing bases, 110–14
    home, 113–14
    leading players for, 114–15
    second, 112–13
    third, 113
Steinbrenner, George, 153
Stengel, Casey, 54, 99, 107–8
Stennett, Rennie, 221
Stocker, Kevin, 220
Stretching
    drill, for pitchers, 69
    for fastballs, 68
Strike zone, defined, 25
Strikes, in Major League Baseball (MLB), 194–98

Suicide squeeze, 24, 101–2
Sullivan, John, 183
Sutter, Bruce, 96
Sutton, Don, 80
Suzuki, Ichiro, 37, 115, 150, 222
Swing, hitting and, 45–46

Tagging up, 105–6
Tampa Bay Rays, 219–21
Tarasco, Tony, 201
Tatis, Fernando, 221
Taveras, Willy, 115
Teams, size of, 13–14
Teixeira, Mark, 8, 107, 152
Temperature, baseball distance and, 75
Tenace, Gene, 41
Terry, Ralph, 43, 88
Texas Rangers, 84
Third base, stealing, 113
Third-base coach, 17
Thomas, Frank, 64, 217
Thome, Jim, 218
Thomson, Bobby, 60, 168, 222
3-and-0 count, 106
Thurber, James, 2
Tiant, Luis, 81, 117
Tidrow, Dick, 124
Ties, in baseball, 15
Toronto Blue Jays, 118
Torre, Joe, 209, 213
Torrez, Mike, 156–57
Total bases (TB), 134
Trammell, Alan, 215
Trillo, Manny, 129
Triple play, defined, 25
Trucks, Virgil, 77
Twin bill, 18
Two-seam grip, 66

Ueberroth, Peter, 165
Umpire's interference, 22–23
Utley, Chase, 150

Valenzuela, Fernando, 166–67, 222
Van Slyke, Andy, 180
Vander Meer, Johnny, 76
Vaughan, Arky, 35
Vaughn, Mo, 104
Versalles, Zoilo, 176
Vision, hitting and, 43–44
Vizquel, Omar, 129
Voiselle, Bill, 223

Wagner, Billy, 95
Waiver trade, defined, 25–26
Wakefield, Tim, 212
Walk, defined, 18
Walker, Larry, 37
Wardlaw, Calvin, 126
Washington Nationals, 84
Washington Senators, 84, 86
Wertz, Vic, 200
Western League, 29
Wettleland, John, 95
Whitake, Lou, 167
White, Frank, 129, 158
Wild pitch, defined, 26
Wild-card era, of baseball, 193–223
Wild-card team, 190–92
Wilfong, Rob, 169
Wilhelm, Hoy, 96, 223
Williams, Bernie, 203, 222
Williams, Gerald, 201
Williams, Matt, 197, 206
Williams, Mitch, 182–83
Williams, Ted, 35–36, 37, 39, 42, 53, 64, 86–87, 100, 107, 169, 198
Wills, Maury, 109, 114, 176
Wilpon, Fred, 94
Wilson, Mookie, 171
Wilson, Willie, 114
Wind, baseball distance and, 75
Winfield, Dave, 129, 222
Wins (W), 135
Wood, Kerry, 210
World Series
   cancellation of 1994, 193–94
   establishment of, 29
   evolution of, 188–89
Worrell, Todd, 165
Wright, Clyde, 119
Wynn, Early, 81

Yastrzemski, Carl, 117, 122, 129, 170, 222
Young, Cy, 30, 77, 188
Yount, Robin, 159

Zimmer, Don, 100, 206
Zimmerman, Ryan, 36
Zito, Barry, 205